"In *You Can Live the Dream,* Nick shows us that you don't have to wait for circumstances to change before you start living the abundant life Jesus offers us all. This book will stir your faith, inspire you to live your purpose, and show you how to walk by faith and not by sight. This is a message of hope we all need right now."

—Christine Caine, founder of A21
and Propel Women

"Nick Nilson's debut book is for anyone who is ready to see your potential from God's perspective. In our struggle, we always have a choice—to give up or to break through our limitations. If you've been feeling stuck and are ready to move forward, *You Can Live the Dream* is a great place to start."

—Steven Furtick, lead pastor of Elevation Church and
New York Times bestselling author of *Crash the
Chatterbox, Greater,* and *(Un)Qualified*

"In a day and age when striving is common, I am grateful for a message that gives us permission to thrive. As someone who has battled the cycle of discontentment in the past, this book is personal for me. I cannot think of anyone better than Pastor Nick to lead us into this mind-set of living our dreams through the power of perspective. He shares this principle with everyone he encounters, not by the words he speaks, but simply by the life he lives. I encourage you to take the time to truly absorb the words on these pages so you can start living the dream!"

—Travis Greene, pastor of Forward City,
recording artist

"If you're ready to stop living in self-doubt and start living your dream right now, this book is for you! Nick shows us how a simple shift in perspective can change everything, and how you don't have to wait for some day far in the future to live your dream life. That day can be today! And in this book, he shows you how!"

—Jamie Kern Lima, *New York Times* bestselling author
of *Believe IT* and founder of IT Cosmetics

"Every page in this book is a joyful invitation to a perspective-changing way of life! The real-life stories, unique insights into God's word, and practical applications to so many areas of my life kept me in it cover to cover! Nick shows us all once again that he's a *now* voice for this moment in history."

—Tauren Wells, platinum-selling
recording artist and pastor

"In Nick Nilson's debut book, we get a heavenly perspective on our earthly circumstances. No matter what we're going through, we can look at the Father and see there's always a way forward with Him! *You Can Live the Dream* is just what you need right now to help you see with that perspective!"

—Derek Carr, four-time Pro Bowl NFL
quarterback for the New Orleans Saints

"I can't count how many times in my life that the very thing that disappointed me was connected to an unexpected upgrade that God was preparing for me. Nick Nilson has provided a powerful, practical guide that will empower you to realize a life beyond what you've dreamed even after a setback."

—Touré Roberts, author,
pastor, entrepreneur

"A good book about dreaming can inspire somebody's soul, but getting to know an actual "dreamer" is like touching a flame that ignites the soul with purpose. I believe Nick Nilson is one of those torch bearers. His faith is contagious, and his hard work, focus, and enthusiasm has always caused those around him to shine with hope. He is not only sharing a book here; he shares his heart and soul in this book. I know that after reading this, you'll be fueled with a clear sense of purpose and passion!"

—Danilo Montero, pastor, author, Latin Billboard Award winner, and two-time Latin Grammy nominee

"We have all had moments of disappointment and exhaustion when it feels like our dreams are at the other end of a long, winding road. Pastor Nick's message will transform your view. He is gifted to inspire. This book will teach you how to embrace a mind-set rooted in emotional well-being so that You Can Live the Dream starting today!"

—Dr. Anita Phillips, LCSW-C, trauma therapist, and author of *The Garden Within*

YOU CAN *LIVE* THE DREAM

TRADING DISAPPOINTMENT AND DISCONTENTMENT
FOR PEACE, JOY, AND FULFILLMENT

NICK NILSON

FaithWords

NASHVILLE · NEW YORK

*To my wife, Summer. Your love, joy, passion,
and faith inspire me. I'm forever grateful I get to
LIVE THE DREAM with you every day.
You saw this book in me long before I did. I love you.*

FaithWords
Hachette Book Group
1290 Avenue of the Americas, New York, NY 10104
faithwords.com
twitter.com/faithwords

First edition: August 2023

FaithWords is a division of Hachette Book Group, Inc. The FaithWords name
and logo are trademarks of Hachette Book Group, Inc.

The publisher is not responsible for websites (or their content) that are not owned
by the publisher.

FaithWords books may be purchased in bulk for business, educational, or
promotional use. For information, please contact your local bookseller or
the Hachette Book Group Special Markets Department at special.markets@
hbgusa.com.

Bible translations used in this book: NIV, NLT, NCB, NET, NKJV, GW, TLB,
ERV, CSB, NCV, NRSV, MSG

Library of Congress Cataloging-in-Publication Data has been applied for.

ISBNs: 9781546004660 (hardcover), 9781546004684 (ebook)

Printed in the United States of America

LSC-C

Printing 1, 2023

CONTENTS

FOREWORD

Nick Nilson is an amazing leader, an insightful minister, and a gifted speaker. For more than seventeen years, Nick has served faithfully and passionately as an indispensable member of Lakewood Church's pastoral leadership team. His love for the Lord is the centerpiece of Nick's life, and he serves as an example of how to lead at work and at home. He is a natural team builder, a great husband and father, and a wonderful friend. I can think of no one better to write about making the most of where you are than Nick.

Sometimes the most difficult place to be is where you are, especially when it's not the place you had hoped to be. We all plan for our future, dream our dreams, and put into motion everything necessary to see our aspirations come to pass, yet, oftentimes, we find ourselves frustrated by the timing of it all. You spend four years in college, study diligently, and graduate with honors only to find that every prospective employer wants you to start at the bottom, perhaps even work for someone who didn't go to college at all.

It's easy to become discouraged. Perhaps, you have worked hard to save for that new home, the one with the backyard, where your children can play. Yet, it seems that every time you save enough for the down payment, something unexpected happens and there goes a chunk of your savings. That can be disheartening to say the least.

It is times like these when you must set your mind and choose to believe that your dreams and your goals are God given. Big dreams require not only faith but patience, as well. The question may not be whether you have faith in God, but whether you're willing to wait on God—and do so with expectancy and joy.

The last part—joy—may be the most difficult for us all, but it is critical if you're going to achieve your dream. Joy comes from knowing that while you are not where you want to be, God has your answer just down the road.

Joy is what keeps you energized and diligent in your efforts. Joy is the reason that that entry level job is not a setback but a challenge to do your best. Joy brings you to your job early each day, before anyone else arrives, and gives you the edge over your competition. Joy shows God that you have not given up on the dream and is why you'll be ready when He places opportunity in your path. Joy is what keeps you looking for that perfect house. It's what drives you to visit open houses, call realtors, and scour the internet even though you're short on the down payment right now.

When the present isn't working out the way you thought it would, staying joyful can be a challenge, especially considering how much easier it is to become disappointed and discouraged. It's difficult to be "living the dream" when things don't seem to be going your way. But living the dream means exactly that—living. It's not a moment; it's a way of living your life. Joy doesn't come and go with your circumstances; it stays with you regardless of your current situation.

You may be asking yourself, "How am I living the dream when I seem to be stuck?" It's a good question, and it's one that Nick answers in this book, *You Can Live the Dream*. Through countless examples and personal experiences, Nick takes you on a journey that is as fulfilling as the destination itself. I encourage you to read this book with expectancy and joy and let today be the day you start living the dream.

—Joel Osteen

INTRODUCTION

You were made to live *the dream*...now. Not next week, not next month, not next year, but right...*now*.

It's easy to think of "the dream" as a destination to which you hope to someday arrive. Perhaps it's when you have a certain amount of money, or you're happily married with two kids, or you have an impressive title next to your name. Or you may think your dream will begin when you're an empty nester, retired with a great 401(k) plan in place, or finally feeling healthy again. From a young age, we are taught that true happiness will be experienced when we arrive at life's mile markers. All of these markers are great, but I want you to see how they can limit you from living "the dream" until you reach those destinations.

I've discovered that we don't have to live long before we find that happiness is far more elusive than reaching a destination. If we expect to find happiness when we finally move into a certain-size house or get the big promotion and salary we worked so hard for, we're going to be disappointed. Don't waste another day "chasing" the dream. Stop limiting and delaying the life you dream of living. It's within your control. In fact, you could be just one perspective shift away from living the life you've always dreamed of living—*now*.

A Destination or a Mind-Set

When I was in my mid-twenties, I began using a phrase that has become a regular part of my vocabulary. When someone asks me how I'm doing, I typically respond: "I'm livin' the dream!" I know, I know, that's nothing new. You've heard this idiomatic expression before. You may have seen it on a T-shirt or on a bumper sticker. People use this phrase to describe a good time with friends. It's been used in ads that show a brand-new house with a shiny Tesla in the driveway. Some empty nesters use it as the slogan for the season of life when their last child has moved out. I see it used often as a perfect caption for the family holiday Instagram post.

In whatever way you have used "livin' the dream" or seen it used, the general meaning assumes an *arrival*, that one's ideal life is being experienced in some way. You have the dream house, the dream job, the dream family, or are experiencing the dream trip.

But for me, it carries a different meaning. It doesn't necessarily mean that I'm where I want to be in my career or that my latest vacation was Instagrammable. It doesn't mean that everything in my life is awesome and going "as planned." It doesn't mean I don't have challenges and struggles that I'm facing and working through. For me, it's a mind-set that I choose to have regardless of what my life looks and feels like on the outside.

"Livin' the Dream" is all about *perspective*. It means that I'm fighting to keep the right perspective on where God has me right now. It's a reminder that each season matters. It's a declaration of my present contentment and confidence in Jesus as well as the future He has in store for me.

The X Factor That Changes Everything

I heard a story about a young man who had trained to become a shoemaker, but there were already two shoemakers in his village. So he packed up his tools and went to another village, looking to start his business and become successful. When he arrived at the village, he saw that no one was wearing shoes. He was so disappointed and frustrated that he turned around and went back to his home village. When his family asked how his business prospects looked there, he said, "Terrible! No one wears shoes there. It's a closed door."

> "Livin' the Dream" is all about *perspective*. It means that I'm fighting to keep the right perspective on where God has me right now.

Soon after he left that village, another shoemaker went to the same village. He saw the same people walking around barefoot. He pulled out his tools and spent the next few weeks showing the people his shoes, demonstrating how they worked, and fitting some villagers with their own custom pair. The news of his shoes spread, and soon his business boomed. When he went back home, his family asked how the business was doing. He replied, "It's fantastic! I can't keep up with the demand. I'm going to have to hire an assistant soon."

Two shoemakers walked into the same village, faced the same circumstances, but they had two different perspectives. One saw an obstacle, a closed door, and walked away. One realized it was the opportunity of a lifetime that could become a flourishing success.

I've seen this same dynamic at work in so many people's lives. I know people who come from the most difficult circumstances, poverty, and dysfunction, yet they've become very successful and fulfilled. And I know many others who grew up in a healthy environment and come from wealthy families yet who are discontent and miserable. What's the difference? What is the X factor that explains the contrast?

Perspective.

The difference is the perspective they have chosen to have on their life and circumstances.

I like what the apostle Paul says about the perspective we should have: "For we live by faith, not sight" (2 Corinthians 5:7 NIV). In other words, faith is all about how we see our lives. It's easy to focus only on what you see happening in your circumstances and allow that to dictate how you think and feel and respond. But I want to encourage you throughout this book to stir up your faith and walk in confidence, believing that God has you where you are for a reason, that He will finish what He started in your life, and He will get you to your destiny. You can't control all the things that happen to you in life, but you can control how you *see* them as well as how you *respond*. Your perspective makes all the difference.

How You See Your Life

"Livin' the Dream" is all about having the right perspective on your life as well as recognizing where you need to change *how* you see your life.

It's about *how* you see your relationships.

It's about *how* you see your finances and opportunities.

It's about *how* you see your past and your future.

It's about *how* you see your problems and setbacks.

You can be in the middle of a financial setback and choose to *see* or believe that God is working it for your good.

You can be in the middle of turmoil at work and have the steady confidence that God is in control.

You can believe God's promise that He will take you through a fiery furnace or den of lions and nothing can keep you from your destiny.

You can choose to see things in your life through eyes of faith and believe that there is opportunity even in the midst of opposition.

The question is whether you believe the difficulties and barriers are keeping you from your destiny, or you see them as occasions for God to show Himself to you. Do you see them as opportunities for growth, as God's means to equip you for what's ahead, or as reasons to be disappointed and to throw the towel in?

I want to encourage you that, with a powerful perspective shift that may defy what you've believed for years, you can begin to say,

"I'm working two jobs, neither of which I planned on doing, but I'm livin' the dream."

"I'm divorced, and it's been painful, but I'm livin' the dream."

"I'm paying off a big debt, but I'm livin' the dream."

"I'm single, and I've been waiting for a long time, but I'm livin' the dream."

It's time to stop chasing the dream and start livin' the dream! Today you can experience *the life* you were designed to live!

You *can* live the dream.

CHAPTER ONE

DROWNING WORMS

Choose the Right Perspective

couldn't wait to take my five-year-old son, Denver, fishing for
the first time. It was so exciting to start a lifelong tradition
with him. I went out and bought the fishing poles, snacks, and
a container of worms for our time together. There was a spot on
a bayou near our house that I thought would give him an easy
introduction to fishing on that summer afternoon. All we had
to do was sit on the concrete bayou bank, bait our hooks with
worms, cast them into the stream, and wait for the fish to strike.
We sat for about thirty minutes, eating sunflower seeds, watching
our lines for a bite, but there was nothing.

   To my surprise, Denver was being fairly patient. Every so

often, he would reel his line in, take the dead worm off, and ask me to help him put on a fresh one. Then he would sling his line back into the water and sit back down. After about an hour of this, Denver remained unshaken and content. I, on the other hand, was done. I wasn't having fun, I was hot, and we hadn't had a single bite. So we packed up our gear and headed home.

To me, this was a major fail. I was hoping this would ignite a bond over fishing that would last us a lifetime. But we caught nothing. We didn't even have a nibble. I was worried that Denver would never want to go fishing again, so I broke the silence and asked him, "Hey, D, what did you think? Did you have a good time today?"

He looked at me and said with a beaming smile, "Dad, I loved drownin' worms with you."

Drownin' worms? What? The whole time he thought we were drowning worms?!!!!

It took everything inside me to keep from bursting into laughter. Since we went through about two dozen worms that day, he thought it was a very successful trip. A few days later, I invited him to drown some worms with me in a different spot, but this time he realized that if he could keep the worms alive, he could also catch some big largemouth bass.

That afternoon with Denver taught me a lot about *perspective.* We were sitting on the same bayou concrete at the same time, seemingly doing the same thing, yet we had two totally different perspectives on our time fishing. From my perspective, we were there to catch fish, and we failed, causing me to chalk it up as a loss. From Denver's perspective, we were there to hang out together and drown some worms. To him, the day couldn't have been better.

Perspective is that powerful.

You could say that Denver and I were looking through two different sets of lenses that day. As a result, we had two entirely different attitudes and reactions to what happened. Your personal perspective will always impact how you respond to everything that happens to you.

See beyond the Circumstances

I believe that the key to living the life God has designed us to live and to becoming all He has created us to be is found in the perspective we *choose* to have. We often can't choose what happens to us, but we can choose how we see it, how we think about it, and in turn how we respond. We can choose to see ourselves and our circumstances as they are, or we can choose to see them through a unique set of faith lenses. The perspective from which you see your life and your experiences can make all the difference.

> *Nothing* has to change in your life for you to experience peace, contentment, and joy.

The reason this is powerful and life-changing is because *nothing* has to change in your life for you to experience peace, contentment, and joy. Your external circumstances don't determine your quality of life. Your perspective of your circumstances does.

A few years ago I was invited to speak at a conference in Southern California. When I arrived at the hotel where I was going to stay for a few nights, we were met by a construction crew as we tried to pull into the entrance. They were doing a lot of roadwork in front of the hotel. Jackhammers were slamming the concrete, cement trucks were lined up and pouring out cement, and project managers were yelling commands through megaphones. It was a loud, chaotic mess.

We were quickly detoured to the side entrance of the hotel to check in. I remember getting off the elevator on the tenth floor, walking into my room, and sliding the balcony door open to a beautiful view of the Pacific Ocean. When I stepped out, I was captivated by the glorious sunset and the calming sounds of rolling waves hitting the sand. Five minutes before, in the same hotel, it was hard to avoid the construction chaos, the diesel exhaust, and the stress of the noise. My address on the map hadn't changed, yet I was experiencing something completely different.

What changed? My elevation. My perspective changed. I had been elevated above the noise, and I was able to see beyond the chaos to something beautiful. That tells me that you can be experiencing chaos all around you and simultaneously experience peace, contentment, and joy. Your problems don't have to go away for you to experience peace. You can experience peace when you elevate your perspective.

We all come into seasons in our life that seem to take the wind out of our sails. It gets chaotic, and the pressure seems overwhelming. The addiction seems unbeatable. The financial burden seems too heavy to carry. The doctor's report just got worse. We feel surrounded and defeated. In those difficult seasons, you have to elevate your perspective, see beyond your current problem, and hope again in God's promises.

When you feel overwhelmed by what's coming against you, the apostle Paul says, "Don't worry about anything; instead, pray about everything. Tell God what you need, and thank him for all he has done. Then you will experience God's peace, which exceeds anything we can understand. His peace will guard your hearts and minds as you live in Christ Jesus" (Philippians 4:6–7 NLT). You might not know that when Paul wrote those words, he was sitting in a Roman prison cell and his life was in the balance. Peace isn't the absence of problems; it's the awareness of God's promise and presence in your life.

I'm not saying that we should ignore reality. The challenges are real, and we need to face them. Faith doesn't ignore the facts; it sees beyond them. Faith helps you see beyond your circumstances. Faith is knowing that the God who is for you is greater than the obstacle that is in front of you.

> Give your circumstances a glance, and give His promise your stare.

In other words, give your circumstances a glance, and give His promise your stare. When you do this, you will begin to experience His peace. The more attention and focus you give to His promise, the more you will experience His peace. It's time to stop giving your problem more attention than His promise. It's time to stop talking about the size of your problem and start talking about the size of your God.

Don't go around thinking and believing that you will never reach your dreams because of a difficulty you are facing. Don't let other people convince you that it's over, that you will never amount to anything, You have to see beyond what's in front of you and beyond the limitations some people have put on you. Get in agreement with God about who you are and what He says about your life. When you begin to do this, you will begin to experience the abundant life He's designed for you to live. Or should I say, "Livin' the dream."

See beyond the Pain

I've found that when I get a change of perspective on a problem and begin to see beyond what's in front of me, I see that God has a purpose even in what is very painful in the moment. Behind every obstacle is an opportunity. Maybe you are facing something painful right now—a difficult situation with your health, a painful season in your family or at work. I want to encourage you that pain never travels alone; it always brings things along with it. If you shift your perspective, you will begin to see that growth, favor, blessings, and other opportunities are attached to these painful seasons and situations. In fact, there are times when closed doors that are painful can be just as important to your purpose and destiny as open doors.

> There are times when closed doors that are painful can be just as important to your purpose and destiny as open doors.

Football has always been my passion. As I blew my birthday cake candles out as a young boy, my one wish was always to become the leading rusher in the NFL. It was my deepest dream, and my brothers and neighbor kids pushed me and fueled that fire. Growing up, we would play tackle football every weekend at the park around the corner from my house. Most of the boys were older and stronger than me, so I learned at an early age how to juke, spin, and run for my life. On Saturdays, we all showed up with our "uniforms" on, which typically were old tattered college or NFL jerseys of our gridiron heroes. Those formidable

Saturdays in the fall were where the dream to play pro football was birthed in me, and I couldn't be talked out of it.

My dad coached my first years of Pop Warner football, and he was the best coach I ever had. I had played running back since I was a kid running away from my brothers on Saturdays, so carrying the ball came naturally. Middle school football seemed to fly by, and by the time I reached the summer before my senior year of high school, I was getting invitation letters from college football programs. Every day, I checked our mailbox for campus invites, excited to plan my next visit and map out my future. This was before MaxPreps and social media. Recruiting was done predominantly in close proximity to the universities. My dream was to play for Michigan State or Wisconsin. I was locked in, working out every day, and getting ready for my senior year under the Friday night lights, when I would hopefully stamp my future at one of these programs.

After three games, I was leading the district in rushing yards and touchdowns, including five in one game. I was leading the district in rushing yards and touchdowns, including five in one game. I was feeling great, and the college scouts' interest in me grew by the week. However, the fourth game of the season felt off from the beginning. It was a back-and-forth, hard-fought first half. When I walked into our locker room at halftime, I had two black eyes from my helmet getting ripped off, and I realized I had a broken thumb. Nonetheless, I had over one hundred yards rushing, and we had the lead.

Halftime concluded, and following the kickoff our coach called "28 Outside Zone," which was my favorite play. I was running at full speed when I got the ball, and when I attempted to make a cut on the wet grass, a defender put his helmet right into the side of my knee and I dropped. Everything from that moment went into slow motion. I knew something was severely wrong with my knee. I had never had a serious injury before, but I could tell this was bad. I couldn't move my leg.

I don't remember every detail of that moment, but I remember that my dad ran out on the field, helped me get up, and walked me to the bench. He sat there with me as the trainers examined my knee. I just sat there in tears with my helmet still on, coming to the realization that my football season was probably over.

I soon learned that I had torn the ACL (anterior cruciate ligament) and MCL (medial collateral ligament) in my knee, which required reconstructive surgery. I was devastated. All the hard work. All the countless workouts, practices, and other sacrifices I had made to see my dream a reality...all for nothing. My childhood dream and hopes for the future felt gone.

At seventeen years old, I had a fight of faith on my hands. I spent many nights during my senior year wondering what my future held. There were many nights of questioning God about where He was that night when I was lying on the wet field at Guilford High's football stadium.

Ever been there? Have you ever had the feeling you get when you invest so much time and effort into something and it doesn't turn out how you imagined? Your business? Your career? Your health? A relationship? You felt certain that something was right, it's what you were supposed to do, everything was going great, and then the door slams shut. It doesn't work out.

It's easy in moments like those to think it's the end based on what we see and think and feel. But in those moments we are also given the opportunity to exercise our faith as at no other time. We can choose to believe that God is going to somehow work everything out for our good. It's easy to have faith when all is well, but what moves Heaven is when you choose to remain in faith in spite of things not working out the way you want.

By the grace of God, though it was very difficult, I chose to *see* my situation through the lens of faith. During that winter, I began to believe that God was going to somehow work the devastating injury for my good. He was going to bring beauty from ashes. I believed that there must be a way for this to become an opportunity for me to grow.

> Have you ever had the feeling you get when you invest so much time and effort into something and it doesn't turn out how you imagined?

Something else really crazy happened as well. Years later, it's still hard for me to explain. But late in that football season, as I watched from the sideline with crutches, God began to shift my heart's desire from football to ministry. Becoming a pastor wasn't something I had ever really thought about. I didn't spend much time in church when I was growing up, and I didn't know much about what a pastor did. But something began to stir in me throughout that winter as I rehabbed my knee. I started to become passionate about the idea of helping people experience the goodness of God and becoming everything God created them to be.

Eventually my knee healed, and college football was still an option on the table. But I chose to turn down those opportunities even though those closest to me thought I was crazy. I knew in my heart that God had purposed me to pursue the ministry and study to become a pastor. I didn't know what it was all going to mean, but I knew I needed to take the step toward it. Now I find myself pastoring and leading in Lakewood Church in Houston,

> God had hit Pause on what I wanted to do and redirected me to what I was made to do

one of the largest churches in America, doing something I never thought would be possible.

Looking back, as hard as that time was in my life, I can thank God for that closed door. In the moment, I didn't see it, and I didn't understand it, but I knew that He was up to something. I don't believe He caused the injury, but He gave me the grace to get through it, and He used it to get me to my destiny. He used it to shift my mind and heart beyond what I saw. It was as if God had hit Pause on what I wanted to do and redirected me to what I was made to do. He knew ultimately where I would be the happiest and most fulfilled.

There was purpose in the pain; it just took me some time to see it and to believe it. It was a blessing in disguise. God will never allow a door to close without already having a bigger and better door ready to open for you. Sometimes you just need to have the right perspective to see it.

See beyond the Opposition

In 2 Kings 6, the house of the prophet Elisha and his servant had been surrounded by a great enemy army in the night. When the servant rose early in the morning and went outside, there were troops, horses, and chariots everywhere. "Oh, sir, what will we do now?" the young man cried to Elisha.

"Don't be afraid," Elisha answered, "for there are more on our side than on theirs." Then he prayed, "O Lord, open his eyes and let him see."

Let's pump the brakes for a second here. Obviously, the servant's eyes were wide open. He could clearly point out the fact that they were about to be destroyed. So what Elisha is really praying here is: "Lord, help him see this from a different perspective. Help him to see beyond the facts, beyond what he sees in the natural." Then the Lord opened the servant's eyes, and when he looked this time, he saw that the hillside around the house was filled with horses and chariots of fire.

The servant had seen half of the reality. In the natural, they were overwhelmingly outnumbered, up against a wall. But when Elisha prayed for him, his vision was elevated, and he saw the angelic forces of Heaven positioned to fight for them. He got a new perspective, and that new perspective completely changed his posture and attitude. As with the servant, God wants you to know that there are more *for* you than there are *against* you.

You may be up against a wall at work or in your finances. It's real. You may be facing a broken relationship that seems beyond restoration or facing an obstacle that's overwhelming and you can't see a way out. I know how hard it is to see beyond it in the natural. I'm asking you to open your eyes of faith as the prophet Elisha did and to see *beyond* your current obstacle and see that God is on your side and He's fighting for you.

After you get informed of a problem and face the reality in front of you, there comes a point when you have to choose a new perspective by exercising your faith and trust in God. This means that you say, "Lord, I'm up against this giant, but I believe You are in control. I didn't expect this negative doctor's report, but I believe that You are working all things for my good. People are gossiping and spreading lies about me at work, but I declare that no weapon formed against me will prosper. I don't know how I'm going to pay next month's rent, but I believe You will meet all my needs according to Your riches in glory. I've made a mistake that I'm not proud of, but I declare that I am a victor and not a victim, and therefore my story ends in victory."

The obstacle may or may not change immediately, but your elevation can. Your perspective of your situation can change. The obstacle may not move, but your hope and trust in God's promises can lift your faith and cause you to see beyond your circumstances and have *hope* that Jesus will bring you out and over what is in front of you.

> Look beyond the giant in front of you and fix your focus on Jesus.

The Scripture says, "With our eyes fixed on Jesus, the author and perfecter of our faith" (Hebrews 12:2 NCB). The assumption is that we all have things that call for our stare, our fixed attention, and permanent focus. The giants, the obstacles, and the challenges we face are real and deserve acknowledgment and a glance, but if you want to overcome them and experience true peace and joy, you have to look beyond the giant in front of you and fix your focus on Jesus.

Following Jesus doesn't necessarily change the circumstances of your life, but following Jesus gives you a *new perspective* of your circumstances. More important, following Jesus gives you a *new perspective* of yourself and your destiny.

That means that the mistake you made doesn't disqualify you. That means that the divorce or the illness or the job loss is not the end of your story. Those things could mean your story is over if you are the author of your story, but you're not. God is. So shift your perspective today. Stop staring at your failures, your past, your hurts, and the giants in front of you, and turn your attention and focus to God, who is the author and finisher of your story.

It's time to shift your perspective and start livin' the dream.

CHAPTER TWO

THE POWER OF LETTING GO

Make Room for the New

am somewhat scarred from an incident that happened to me when I was ten years old.

My older brother, Adam, and I had begged my mom for years to buy us a dirt bike. Well, much to our surprise, she finally gave in, and one summer morning she woke us up, told us to hurry and get dressed, because we were going to go test-drive a motorcycle! We were so excited as we pulled up the long driveway to the seller's house. The minibike was parked outside the garage when we arrived. It was more of a road bike with smaller tires, taller handle bars, and a banana seat with "El Tigre" written on the back of it. My brother hopped on it first, and without hesitating, he pulled the throttle and took off down the driveway. I watched as he made it look effortless, weaving in and out of the trees of the yard. He rode the bike back to me, brought it to an abrupt stop, looked at me, and said, "Be very careful when you start. It has some power when you hit the throttle." Then he handed the bike over to me.

It was my turn. I had never actually ridden a minibike like this before. I sat down on the bike, very nervous, but I was anxious to introduce myself to El Tigre. I took a deep breath, gripped the handle bars, pulled the throttle, and the tiger took off! Next thing I knew, El Tigre had almost completely thrown me off the bike, and I was clutching the grips by the tips of my fingers. As gravity was pulling me back, I instinctively tightened my grip. The only problem was that the grip is also the throttle, so by holding on, I was causing the bike to go even faster. I started swerving all over the place, with my legs dragging the ground and kicking dirt with every jerk of the bike. Then I suddenly heard my mom and my brother screaming,

"LETTTTT GOOOOO! LET GO OF THE BIKE!"

Just before hitting a huge maple tree, with my ten-year-old life flashing before my eyes, I let go of the bike, which went crashing into a fence. I ended up taking a few barrel rolls across the grass and miraculously only ended up with a couple of scrapes and bruises. Thankfully, there was only minimal damage to the minibike, but there was a mutual understanding that we had to buy it after the incident.

El Tigre taught me a valuable lesson that day. Holding on, in that moment, meant disaster for me. It was frightening, and almost surreal, but I'm so glad I chose to let go of the bike that day. I've learned that there are so many things in our lives that, if we hold on to them, can limit our growth, delay our destiny, and keep us from God's best. For many people, there are relationships or even mistakes that are hindering them from being their best, simply because they haven't let go of them.

Letting Go Of the Past

In the book of Exodus, we read that God's special people, the Israelites, had been oppressed in slavery for hundreds of years in Egypt, under ruthless work conditions and heavy demands from Pharaoh. The Israelites who knew of the covenant and promise that God had made with them as a nation began to cry out to God in desperation. God heard their cry and assigned Moses to lead Israel out of Egypt. Through a series of astonishing plagues upon the Egyptians and miracles for the Israelites, God delivered them. However, not long after God parted the Red Sea, brought them through on dry ground, and was leading the Israelites through a wilderness, they began to complain against Moses and Aaron. They said, "Our Egyptian slavery was far better than dying out here in the wilderness. Why did we ever leave Egypt? There's nothing good to eat here and nothing to drink."

I can imagine an Israelite man being hungry, thirsty, hot, and uncomfortable in the desert, with an unhappy wife and unhappier children in their tent, picturing the home he left behind in Egypt. His past life is suddenly looking so good in his mind. He's forgetting the bitter slavery and the bondage, and he's only remembering how predictable it was. He's craving the familiar.

Here's what's crazy. The journey to the Promised Land that should have taken weeks, maybe a few months max, took the Israelites forty years! Yes, forty *years*. Their destiny was delayed. Why?

They wouldn't let go.

The Israelites were on their way to the promise, and some

tests came. They got tired of God's daily supply of food, didn't know where their water would come from, didn't like living in tents, and all they could see was a barren wilderness. When they hit some rough terrain, the thought of turning around and going back began to sound so good. It's true that when you can't see the future, it's easy to dwell in the past. When you can't see your husband, it's easy to go back to the last guy. When the present doesn't seem to be fruitful, the past seems to be better than it really was. When you can't see your future, it's easy to hold on to the past.

> You may be just one faith release away from receiving something greater that has your name on it.

We all have a promise from God for a new land, a new level, a new territory—it's our destiny. We also have an Egypt—a past, a place where we are coming from. Your Egypt might be an unhealthy relationship that you got out of, but now you're in a season of loneliness and that old relationship looks appealing. Maybe it's a bad habit that God freed you from, but as you've been scrolling on social media, it begins to look so enjoyable. Maybe it's an old job in a different city that you know you needed to leave, but it's looking so good from afar.

The Israelites were *next door* to their Promised Land, but they couldn't receive it because they wouldn't let go of their past. You may be right next door to your promised land, right next door to a new season of freedom and peace, but you are still holding on to the past. You have to release the past so you can receive the new beginning that God has for you. You may be just one faith release away from receiving something greater that has your name on it.

You may not know what tomorrow holds, but you can rest when you know Who holds it. You may not see the promise, but you can trust the Promise Giver. What's behind you is no comparison to what God has in store for you.

New Beginnings

I have always tried to be a good person. My parents taught me from a young age to love and respect everyone. They consistently pushed me to work hard and excel in school and sports. While my dad was highly involved in my life, it was more difficult for my mom, because after my parents divorced when I was three, she moved about thirty minutes away. Before my mom married my dad, she had two children, Kris and Heather, whom my father adopted. A few years later, my brother, Adam, was born, and I followed as the youngest, born on Christmas Day. And yes, growing up I always felt shaded on presents. "Here's a gift for both your birthday *and* Christmas." If your birthday is near a holiday, I can feel your pain.

When my parents divorced after seven years of marriage, my mom got custody of Heather and Kris, and my dad got custody of Adam and me. We would visit our mom every other weekend. My dad remarried a few years after the divorce, and my stepmom, Debbie, brought two of her own children into the home. Growing up in a blended home was normal for us. My dad and stepmom did the best they could to provide for us in every way. They made a lot out of a little. Hand-me-downs, knockoff cereals, and corn dogs. Sunday family nights were a must. My dad would pick up a pizza and rent the scariest movie he could find. It wasn't unusual after *Friday the 13th Part XIX* for my dad to turn the power off in the house for a very intense game of hide and seek. I may have peed a little in my pants a few times hiding from my dad in a closet. The fact that he was 6 feet 3, 220 pounds, and wore his Dickies' work uniform for added effect contributed to my petrification.

By the time I'd reached high school in Beloit, Wisconsin, I was experimenting with drugs and alcohol. They were all around me—at home, at school, in my neighborhood. It was the social norm. During my ninth grade year at Beloit Memorial High, I wanted to experience living and spending more time with my mom for the remainder of my high school years, so I talked with both my parents. This was a very difficult decision, but the high school to which I would transfer had a great football program, which was more in line with my football aspirations. So I moved thirty minutes away to Roscoe, Illinois.

I went from a neighborhood and high school that were extremely diverse to a school that was predominantly white. This was a huge change for me. I did my best to adjust to my new surroundings, acclimating into the party scene and trying to excel in academics, sports, and popularity at Hononegah High.

During my junior year, I met a guy named Dan Hade at one of our first varsity basketball practices. I had seen Dan a few times at parties. I can't explain it, but there was just something different about him. He had a joy about him that was unique. On and off the court, he lived with a contentment that appealed to me. He was a handsome guy who could have easily hooked up with girls, but he didn't seem fixated on the things that obsessed most of us on the team. One day Dan asked if I wanted to come over to his house and hang before our home basketball game, which started a tradition. Dan and I would hang before every game, often binge-ing on Cheetos and PlayStation and sleeping on his couch. Dan was cool. He could hoop, he was funny, and he seemed to have his life sorted out and lived for a purpose.

One summer night the phone rang, and I saw Dan's name come up on the caller ID box. (Remember those? If you don't, google them.) Dan and I caught up for a few minutes, and then he invited me to City First's youth summer camp. This was Dan's church, and he was going to the camp in a few weeks. By this time, I knew Dan was passionate about his faith, and I just thought it was good for *him*, something *he* needed. But now he was inviting me to join him on a weeklong experience. I was unsure about it and told him that if I didn't have any football commitments, I would go. That was actually an excuse. I was almost positive I had a football camp or a college visit to attend every week that summer. When Dan followed up with me a few days later, I checked my calendar and was shocked that his camp fell on the only week I had free. I reluctantly committed.

Next thing you know, I'm traveling in a car with Dan and a few others to Spencer Lake, Wisconsin. On the way up, we decided to see how many Mountain Dews and how much candy we could consume. That was a bad idea. As soon as we arrived, I walked down to the lake and threw up. I felt horrible and went straight to my bunk to sleep and missed the first night of camp. We spent the next day swimming and launching off the Blob in the lake and playing sand volleyball. It was so much fun. That night we went to the evening service, which was different for me. People were jumping, lifting their hands, and singing with all their heart. I had never been in a faith environment like this.

I don't remember a lot about the service or the sermon, but I will never forget how it ended. As the pastor closed, he asked if anyone wanted to receive Jesus as their personal Lord and Savior.

He talked about how you could know about God, yet still be missing out on the relationship He intended to have with you. My heart was pounding. As he spoke, I had an overwhelming urge to respond. I had never asked Jesus to forgive me of my sins and come into my life and be my personal Savior. Up until then, I thought just believing that there was a God and being a good person were enough to get to Heaven. I prayed whenever I needed God, when I was in a bind or wanted to play great before a game. That night I walked down to the front of the stage to make Jesus the center of my life. I knew I needed grace for my sins. I wanted a new beginning, and I got one. On June 18, 1998, my life changed forever. I let go of

> On June 18, 1998, my life changed forever. I let go of my past, all my mistakes and sins, and received the grace of God for the first time.

my past, all my mistakes and sins, and received the grace of God for the first time. I went to bed that night experiencing a peace in my heart I had never experienced before. I felt the contentment and joy I had witnessed in Dan's life. Jesus wasn't this far-off, religious figure who was irrelevant and boring. He wasn't just someone else's Lord and Savior. He was my Savior. He was my Lord, and He had just changed the trajectory of my life.

The next few days at camp, I began to learn what it meant to walk with Jesus. I learned that my faith wasn't based on religion, but it was a relationship with God. Religion says, "Fix yourself, then come to God." The gospel says, "You belong long before you learn to behave. Jesus loves you as you are, and it's only through Him that you can change and become all He has created you to be." This was the first time I read that Jesus said, "The thief comes only to steal and kill and destroy; I have come so that they may have life, and may have it abundantly" (John 10:10 NET). I had been searching for an abundant life in all the wrong places. Things would make me feel good in the moment, but I realized it all faded. Yes, I had been a comparatively good guy, successful with lots of friends, but I was empty. That week shifted the entire perspective of my life. I had a new way of looking at my life, through a lens of faith, and it changed everything.

The week ended with an opportunity to get baptized in the lake. When I learned what it meant, I was all in! Water baptism is the outward expression of an inward change. Jesus had found me and opened my eyes to His love and purpose for my life. I wanted to go public and put the past behind me. So alongside dozens of other teenagers, I walked down to the lake on that last day and got water baptized. I picked up the first rock I could grab from the lake bottom, so I would never forget that moment.

I drove home a new person. At seventeen years old, I began to live the dream—not because anything had changed on the outside of my life, but everything had changed on the inside. I stepped into a relationship with God and realized that He had a plan and purpose for my life, that He had shaped me to fulfill a destiny, and that He was going to shape me into the man He had designed me to be. This is the abundant life that Jesus came to give you and me! My perspective of my life had completely changed. This is what livin' the dream is all about. Maybe you feel you are not good enough for God to love you. Maybe, like me, you know

> I began to live the dream—not because anything had changed on the outside of my life, but everything had changed on the inside.

about God but have never really stepped into a relationship with Him. Maybe you are at the lowest place you've ever been in your life and you're looking for hope. I have good news! Today can be a new beginning for you. You are not reading this by accident. Express your faith in Jesus and allow His love and grace to change you from the inside out. I'm a living witness that giving your heart to Jesus is the best and most important decision you can make in your life!

Make Some Room

Where God is taking you is so much more important than where you've been. But if you're always looking back at the past, you won't see what's ahead. Just think about your car windshield as compared to the rearview mirror. The windshield is so much larger because what's in front of you is so much more important than what's behind you. In the same way, your future is more important than your past. It's fine to remember the good moments, but you can't live there.

I'll never forget when my son, Denver, lost his first tooth. One morning he came rushing down the stairs from his bathroom and exclaimed, "Dad, what am I going to do?" He opened his mouth and pointed to a gap in the center of his smile. Holding the tooth in his hand like it was precious, he cried out, "My teeth are all falling out!" He thought he was going to lose them all permanently. The problem was that Denver couldn't see or feel the permanent tooth underneath. I explained to him that when one tooth falls out, another stronger, better tooth grows in over time. He was relieved to know that another tooth was actually waiting to grow in and just needed some room. After he discovered that, Denver was anxious to help the process along and make room. We often caught him moving, wiggling, and trying to shake loose as many baby teeth as possible. Letting go was no longer a problem.

I wonder how many blessings assigned to us are looking for space. Looking for room.

What's still taking up space in your life that needs to be let go of in order to make room for the new things God wants to do? Unforgiveness? A negative mind-set? An unhealthy relationship? A past mistake? Whatever it is, God is waiting for you to make room so He can replace and fill that space with the bigger and better things He has in store.

> What's still taking up space in your life that needs to be let go of in order to make room for the new things God wants to do?

It's time to let go of the past hurt, so you can walk into the promise of freedom.

It's time to let go of what didn't work out, so you can receive the promotion that's coming.

It's time to make some room for the better things God has prepared for you.

Plows and Coats

In 1 Kings 19, the prophet Elijah was ready to pass his mantle of leadership to Elisha. It says that when Elijah passed by Elisha, he "threw his mantle on him." This symbolized a new season when God was bringing promotion and opening a new door for Elisha. After Elijah transferred his cloak, heavy with destiny, onto Elisha's shoulders, Elisha did something interesting. Verse

21 says that he left Elijah, went back to his home, took his yoke of oxen with which he had been plowing his fields, and slaughtered them. He then burned his plowing equipment to cook the meat and gave it to the people to eat. Then he set out to follow Elijah and became his servant.

> What plows do you need to burn in order to step into all that God has for you?

What's interesting is that Elisha's oxen as well as his plowing equipment were his means to make a living. This was how he derived his income. His family and his neighbors must have thought he had lost his mind, that he was being irresponsible. But Elisha had a different perspective. He wanted to make sure that as he stepped into his destiny, there was nothing to come back to, or even to look back to. He knew that there was a high probability that he would eventually run into some tough times. He knew that obstacles were inevitable, and he would be tempted to return to his past. The oxen and plowing equipment would look appealing. So he made a decision to slaughter the oxen and burn the plows. He dealt with it. His destiny required him to let go of the present and in faith to step into the unexpected.

As was true for Elisha, today can mark a new chapter for you, a new season. What got you to this point in your life may not be able to go with you into your future. God has another level of maturity for you, and reaching that level may require you to let go of some things. What plows do you need to burn in order to step into all that God has for you? For some people, that might mean to stop hanging around people at work who gossip. It might mean to stop hanging around places that lure you to compromise. It might mean dealing with the insecurity that keeps you from the greater opportunities that are in front of you. It's time to do as Elisha did and get rid of what you know you can't go back to, so you can step into what's in front of you.

In Mark 10, Jesus was leaving the city of Jericho and was surrounded by a great crowd of people. A blind man name Bartimaeus was sitting by the road begging. When he heard that Jesus of Nazareth was passing by, he began to cry out, "Jesus, Son of David, have mercy on me!" Many in the crowd became annoyed with Bartimaeus and told him to be quiet, but he shouted all the more, "Son of David, have mercy on me!" Jesus heard the man, stopped, and said, "Call him." When they told the beggar that Jesus was calling him, the Scripture says, "Bartimaeus threw aside his coat, jumped up, and came to Jesus." Why did Mark even mention Bartimaeus's coat when he wrote this Gospel? Why was that significant? It's because this coat was issued by the government and qualified Bartimaeus to beg and collect donations. This coat was the only means by which he could survive. When Bartimaeus discarded this coat, he was making a bold declaration. He was saying that he no longer needed this coat. He was not going to be identified by it as a beggar anymore. Jesus had come, and he believed he was going to be healed. He would no longer be dependent on the government or live off donations. He was going to depend on Jesus and live the dream. What's interesting is that Bartimaeus let go of his coat before he even got to Jesus. I believe this move of faith caught the attention of Jesus and moved Him to release power and favor in his direction.

Letting go takes the limits off God. The risk is not in letting go, but in not launching into the new season of greater things. The real risk is living in mediocrity and never changing, never maturing and reaching your full potential simply because you didn't let go. In the midst of your uncertainty, remember that your future and your destiny don't rest on your résumé or past performance; they rest on God's grace and His goodness. We see so many people in the Bible who let go of things to follow Jesus as Bartimaeus did. For some it was fishing nets, for another it was a coat, and for another it was a tax-collecting booth. Those were "plows" being burned. Don't let your "Egypt" keep you from your destiny. Greater joy, influence, and freedom all start with letting go and choosing to burn some plows. But remember that the burning may take longer than a day. It may take weeks, months, or a season as you surrender something to God. I believe as you do, His Spirit and power will transform you and prepare you for what's ahead.

> Don't let your "Egypt" keep you from your destiny.

Let Go Of the Mistakes

When my son, Denver, was ten, I had the opportunity to help coach his tackle football team. I learned that the first key to coaching ten-year-olds in football is to make sure they all remember to use the bathroom *before* the game. We had a few near mid-game accidents. The second key is the constant need to remind the boys to forget about their last mistake. In football, as well as any other sport, we all make mistakes, and when you're ten years old, you make a lot of them. You miss a block or a tackle, fumble or drop a pass. When these kids make a mistake, it's difficult for them to forget it. They dwell on it for the rest of the game. This was frustrating because we lost some games or didn't play to our full potential, not because the other team was more talented, but because our kids simply couldn't overcome their mistakes. Our players were so fixed on what was behind them that they couldn't fully step into what was ahead of them.

No matter what your age is, chances are that you've made mistakes in your life that have had the same effect on you. You've had some plays, some quarters, some seasons in your life that were filled with mistakes, an addiction, or maybe a divorce, and it's been hard for you to move forward. You haven't let go of them, and as a result, you're not hopeful for the future, you've talked yourself out of the great things God has for you, and you're not living up to your full potential. Today is the day you can quit beating yourself up and reliving past mistakes. Don't let that failure, that habit, or that season define you. Those decisions and seasons don't define you. God does. He doesn't call you a divorcée, an addict, or a dropout.

> You can't change what's behind you, but you can do something about what's in front of you.

He calls you His child. It's time to see yourself as He does. You can't change what's behind you, but you can do something about what's in front of you. So forgive yourself, let go, and move on.

If you are having a hard time letting go of a mistake, consider what the apostle Peter went through. At the beginning of Jesus' ministry, He saw Peter on a beach by the Sea of Galilee and called him from his fishing lifestyle and commissioned him into his God-given purpose. "Follow Me, and I will make you fishers of men" (Matthew 4:19 NKJV). Peter was all in. He put his nets down and began to chase his purpose. He became one of Jesus' disciples, walking with him, witnessing miracle after miracle, learning, being equipped to lead. He essentially became one of Jesus' right-hand guys.

Then the unimaginable happened.

In John 18, while Jesus awaited His trial and verdict, Peter was standing on the outskirts of the courthouse on a cold, brisk night. To keep warm, the guards and a servant girl built a fire, but not just any type of fire. The word *anthrakia* is used, which means a charcoal fire, and it's an important detail as you'll soon see. It's around this charcoal fire on a cold night that Peter would be asked three times if he was one of Jesus' disciples. Three times he would deny even knowing Jesus, something he swore he would never do.

Ever been there? Ever done something you swore to God you would never do?

You told God you would never cuss the next time a person cuts you off in traffic, but you do.

You told God you wouldn't go to that website again, but you do.

You told God it would just be one drink next time, but it's not.

You told God you would give the next time you had the opportunity, but you don't.

Ever been there…with Peter? We all have.

The God Who Comes Back

Peter made a huge mistake, not just once but three times, while Jesus was sentenced to death on a cross, was crucified, died, and was buried. As a result, Peter was overwhelmed not only with the death of His mentor, but also with the guilt and bitter shame of his denial. But on the third day, Jesus rose from the dead, and He appeared to His disciples twice over a span of days. Despite that, Peter made the decision to go fishing in John 21. He *went back* to his old lifestyle. He allowed the feeling of inadequacy and failure to push him back into living in mediocrity.

Now, it's interesting that Jesus could have done a lot of things in the short window of time He spent on earth before He ultimately ascended to Heaven, but He had one stop He was determined to make. There was one person with whom He had to spend more time. There was one person He had to connect with and restore. So He headed to the beach nearby where Peter and six of the other disciples had spent the whole night fishing and caught nothing. These weren't novice fishermen. They'd been doing this their whole lives, but this night they were skunked. Nothing. I imagine that during the night when it was quiet and there was nothing in the nets, Peter was lost in his thoughts. He began to once again dwell upon his failure. He'd been called to something great, to be a fisher of men, but he had drifted from his purpose. I imagine that was a rough night for Peter. He was tired, cold, frustrated, and hungry.

Early in the morning, the disciples saw a figure on the shoreline. The man from the beach yelled, "Throw the net on the right side of the boat." With nothing to lose, they did, and the net immediately filled up! To be exact, they caught 153 large fish. That's a lot of fish. John immediately shouted from the back of the boat, "That's a Jesus move!" Peter couldn't believe it and impulsively jumped in the water and began to swim the one hundred yards to the shore. But as he was swimming, he began to catch the smell of something burning. It was a fire, and the smell of smoke carried out into the sea. Now, this wasn't any fire. This was a fire that Jesus had taken time to prepare by Himself. And it wasn't just any type of fire. John is very specific in describing it with the word *anthrakia*. There it is again, a charcoal fire. This was odd because being by the Sea of Galilee, there would be plenty of dried-out driftwood to build a fire, and it would have been easier, more convenient. But John definitely wants us to know that Jesus didn't just prepare any fire. He went out of His way to prepare a charcoal fire.

As Peter was swimming, you better believe that he recognized that distinct smell, because the sense of smell is one of the most powerful memory triggers. A certain aroma can trigger memories and take you back decades to an event associated with that smell—a moment, a place, a person. Peter smelled the charcoal, and it had to trigger a memory. The only other time the word *anthrakia* is used in the New Testament is to describe the fire where Peter failed. The smell alone ushered in flashbacks of what had happened at that fire. He smelled his own denial again, and now He saw the One whom he had denied. When Peter got to shore, Jesus was already cooking fish and bread on the charcoal fire.

> We serve a God who comes back to us. He comes back to you. Even when you are at your worst, He comes back!

You have to realize that Jesus didn't have to come back to get Peter. He *wanted* to restore him. He doesn't have to come back to us after our mistakes, but He wants to. He didn't come back to remind Peter of his mistake; He came back to remind Peter that His love was *bigger* than his mistake. He was redefining him. Jesus was saying, "I know what you did around that fire, but forget it. I want you to remember what is happening around *this* fire. I want you to remember that I came back to you, and that I love you." We serve a God who comes back to us. He comes back to you. Even when you are at your worst, He comes back!

The God Who Restores

After the disciples ate that morning, Jesus invited Peter to take a private walk. They walked toward the net still filled with the huge catch of fish that they had dragged onto the shore. As they approached it, Jesus asked Peter three times, "Do you love Me?" One translation says, "Peter, do you love Me more than these?" (John 21:15 NKJV). Scholars who have spent their lives studying the Gospel of John debate what the word *these* refers to. Most believe that Jesus was not referring to the disciples. Most believe *these* represented the huge catch of fish. In other words, Jesus was saying, "Do you love Me more than your past? More than what you are allowing the shame and failure to push you to?"

Three questions for three denials, which is a beautiful picture of grace. Jesus was reinstating Peter. He was redefining him! He was inviting him to no longer allow his mistakes to define him. "Peter, do you love Me more than these? Because I love you more than your worst mistake." In other words, "I know you love Me, Peter, so let's move on from your failure. Stop living in regret and shame, allowing it to rob you of your future."

One fire represents failure; the other represents his future. We all have a choice that follows every mistake we make, a choice that our future ultimately depends upon, and that's what we do with the grace of God. Isaiah 61:3 says that God wants to give you beauty for ashes. You can't receive the beauty if you don't let go and give God your ashes. This is what Jesus was asking Peter to do. Today, give God your ashes. Give Him your worst mistake. Quit holding on to it and allowing it to distract you from your purpose. Peter finally did, and look what happened! In just a matter of days following the second fire, Peter moved forward and preached on the day of Pentecost. When he did, three thousand people gave their lives to Jesus. The church exploded and became the unstoppable force of love that it is today.

I wonder what's waiting on the other side of grace for you. What purpose, what opportunity, what new relationship is there?

Whatever you feel disqualifies you or negates you from your purpose has been covered by His grace. Maybe you find yourself between the two fires today? Maybe you're stuck between a mistake and your future. This is God's way of coming to you and saying, "You're forgiven. Let go of the mistake, shake off the shame, and let's move on together."

Life Is Better in His Hands

I've found that it's not just our past and our mistakes that are hard to let go of, but it's also our need to be in control.

When our daughter, Haven, got her driver's permit, she was excited to get her license and so were we. The thought of her being able to drive herself places thrilled us. However, to get her license, she had to log a certain amount of hours driving, which meant Summer and I had to take her out driving. I can't recall another time in my life when I needed to exercise more faith. Why didn't any other parent warn me about this? I was sitting on the passenger side of my car, with no control! I had given complete control of the vehicle to my fifteen-year-old daughter. I was at the mercy of her decisions. To say that my hands gripped the seat is an understatement. I had one hand locked on the dash and the other glued to the seat. Why was this so hard? It's simple. I went from feeling like I was in control to having no control, and it was scary.

> Maybe you find yourself between the two fires today?

But the truth is that control is an illusion. None of us are really in control of anything. God is. All we can control is how we respond to things that happen in life. I'm learning that the more I try to hold on and control everything in my life, the worse things become and the more anxious I get. On the other hand, it's amazing what can change in your life when you simply choose to put it in God's hands.

Look at it this way. A basketball in my hands can do some things. It can be dribbled, get shot, perhaps score eight points in a local men's basketball league. What if we took that same ball and put it in the hands of LeBron James? I promise you that *a lot* more could happen with it—dunks, triple doubles, MVPs, championships. In my hands, the ball doesn't seem like much. It's worth about $19. A basketball in the hands of LeBron James, however, is worth millions, and it can do a lot more.

> Control is an illusion. None of us is really in control of anything. God is.

You can try to hold on to things and try to fix your problems all on your own, or you can put all your trust in other people to sort things out. You may experience some success, some fulfillment, but you will never reach your full potential. You will never experience the life of purpose God has designed for you. However, if you choose to put your life in God's hands, you'll be amazed by what He can do with it. I wonder what God could do with your finances. With your marriage. With your challenges at work. The same hands that created the world can change *your* world.

You just have to *let go*.

One Hundred and Livin' the Dream

I recently visited some of my family in Wisconsin. Anytime I'm in town, I try to stop by my grandma's apartment to spend

time with her. I cherish these moments. My Grandma Phyllis
is the queen of the Nilson side of the family. She's always smiling, always in a great mood, and never
complains. She's ninety-eight years old
and still as sharp as ever. She has sixteen
grandkids and twenty-nine (and counting)
great-grandkids. What's amazing is that
she knows every name and has memorized
every birthday. Can you believe that? I
can't even remember my own kids' birthdays sometimes!

> Life is too short to hold on to mistakes and offenses.

I felt compelled on this visit to ask her some serious questions
since I never know if it will be my last time with her. After visit-
ing for a while, catching her up on the latest news with my kids
and answering all the questions she had about my life, it was my
turn. I asked, "Grandma, you always seem to be positive. You are
always happy. I know you have been through loss, struggles, wars,
and now a pandemic. How do you do it? After living ninety-eight
great years, what advice would you give someone?"

She thought about it for a moment, then she replied, "I just try
not to get stuck in the past, looking back. I try to stay focused on
the future and what's ahead. Life is too short to hold on to mistakes and offenses. What you need to hold on to is your faith and
hope. I don't dwell on troubles and challenges. I dwell on God's
goodness and the good things He's done."

Those words sank deep into my soul that day.

It was hard not to hold back tears. I believe one of the reasons
my grandma is almost one hundred, healthy, and flourishing, is
because of her mind-set and perspective on life. You can't live the
dream now while holding on to what didn't work out in your past.
Don't let guilt about your past keep you from living the life God

has for you right now. It doesn't matter if you are twenty or a hundred. Choose today to let go of the past so you can enjoy the present and the future God has in store for you. I believe as you begin to make these bold moves of faith, you will experience new levels of peace, growth, and contentment in your life!

CHAPTER THREE

PROGRESS OVER PERFECTION

Celebrate the Good on the Way to Great

Recently Summer and I had to redo some of our backyard landscaping. We put in some new trees, shrubs, flowers, and bushes. We were excited to see our plan take shape and watch some of the plants start to blossom and bloom into color. But after a few weeks, some of the trees didn't look healthy. Summer would come in from watering and checking them out and say, "Nick, the trees look like they're dying. We need to call a landscaper and ask for advice." I kept reminding her, "They're okay. They've just been transplanted and gone through a lot. They'll be fine."

A few days later, I thought the trees looked worse than ever. I said, "Summer, I think you're right. We need to call the landscaper." I can't tell you how many times we went back and forth on what to do with our plants. We had a landscaper come and inspect them six times, only to be reminded that growth is a process that takes *time*. The roots needed time to settle and begin drawing nutrients. The leaves needed time before they would look good again. He kept assuring us that although nothing appeared to be changing, a lot was happening beneath the ground's surface. Life was sprouting up, and despite how they appeared, progress was taking place. We learned that it takes *time* for them to become what they were designed to be.

> Are there dreams, relationships, or people whom you have given up on simply because they were not happening, changing, or progressing as fast as you wanted?

I wonder how many things we give up on in our lives because they're taking too much time. Are there dreams, relationships, or people whom you have given up on simply because they were not happening, changing, or progressing as fast as you wanted? I encourage you not to quit on someone or something because it's not changing as quickly as you hoped. Better yet, don't be too hard on yourself because you aren't changing or improving in areas as fast as you hoped. Growth is a process, and my challenge to you is to learn to enjoy the process, not just endure it. Learn to celebrate even though things aren't where you want them to be in your life.

Celebrate the Partial Victories

In Genesis 1, it took God six days to do something He could have done in a moment. Think about that. He could have spoken the word and all of creation would have appeared instantly and been in full operation. But no, He took six days. We see that God establishes a pace and a pattern for the created to follow. He established this very important principle: It takes time for good things to take shape, transform, and develop.

God also did something else that was important in this passage. On the first day, when He created the Heavens and the Earth, He said, "Let there be light," and light came. At the end of that first day, God said, "It is good." The Earth was formless and empty—no oceans, no sky, no animals. It was an unfinished product, but at the end of that day, God said, "It is good." On the second day, God separated the waters from the sky, but there were still no fish or birds, no sun or moon, no people, yet at the end of that day He said, "It is good." It was the same thing at the end of days three, four, and five. Creation was incomplete, the miracle was unfinished, but five times God said, "It is good." On the sixth day, when God completed creation, this time He said, "It is *very* good." He was establishing another important principle: If you don't learn to see the good in the unfinished, you'll never get to *very* good.

God was teaching and modeling something for us as we are growing and becoming everything He's designed us to be. *Enjoy the good. Thank God for the good. Be grateful for the good.* I know you aren't fully where you want to be. I know there are changes you still want to see in your life and in those you love. Things in your career may not be where you want them to be. There may be a lot that's unfinished in your life, but thank God for the good, for what has been done. Thank God for the victories and changes you have seen.

The mistake we often make is to wait for the total victory to celebrate. "When I get over this illness, or when this situation clears up, or when I break free from this addiction, then I'll

> You have to celebrate the good on the way to great.

celebrate." No, the key to seeing it come to fulfillment is to celebrate partial victories along the way. You have to celebrate the good on the way to great.

So you're not totally out of debt, but you paid off one credit card. Celebrate it. You haven't lost all the weight, but you lost five pounds. Celebrate that victory. You haven't received your college degree, but you finished one year. Celebrate that progress. When you celebrate your partial victories, when you are grateful for the good, it's only a matter of time before God takes you to *very good*.

Have you noticed how we begin our lives on a pace and pattern of growth and progress? The first time a baby rolls over or makes a cooing sound, the cameras come out and videos are posted on social media for the whole world to see. A child takes his or her first step, and the parents run circles around their living room in celebration. The child didn't complete a marathon or win a gold medal. It was one step. One word. One tooth. As parents, we can't help but celebrate every little win as our kids grow. So why do we stop as we continue to grow and progress? Why do we stop celebrating along the way? Often as we experience life, it's easy to get so focused on the completion, on getting to a goal, that we miss or take for granted the small wins in our lives along the way. Perhaps you're struggling with anxiety attacks and hoping to be completely free from them, and you've had only one in three weeks. That's a partial victory, a small win for you. Celebrate it. Maybe you didn't make the big sale that you worked so hard for, but you made two small sales. Guess what? That's a win. Don't go around complaining about what you didn't get. Be grateful for the small wins.

Sports have taught me a lot about this. Throughout games, you see athletes celebrate on the way to the ultimate goal. I was watching the recent NBA finals. The goal of each player and team before the start of each season is to win the championship. That's the dream. As I watched the first game of the seven-game final series, a player got fouled, went to the free throw line, and made his first free throw. What happened? Every team member leaned over, high-fived, and celebrated with him. There were three quarters left in the game, and it was only game one of seven. Why celebrate? This was a professional athlete who should make a simple free throw. The shot did not win the championship or even the game. But professional athletes understand the importance of celebrating a small victory on the way to the ultimate goal. Players and teams intentionally stop and celebrate these small wins—the made free throw, the first down, the base hit. Why?

> It's good to celebrate where you are while God changes you into the person He ultimately wants you to be.

This builds momentum. It generates strength and confidence in the player and the team. It's celebrating *progress*.

I'm not saying to ignore your failures or mistakes and not deal with your weaknesses. I'm saying you have to look for the improvements you're making and thank God for that good. When you haven't broken the smoking addiction but you cut it down to ten cigarettes a day, that's a made free throw to be celebrated. When you cut down from six to three Oreos before going to bed, that is good. Pat yourself on the back, but don't celebrate with Blue Bell ice cream. (My Texas family will understand.) When someone cut you off on the road, you just smiled, waved, and kept driving rather than giving them a friendly gesture. For some people that's no big deal, but for you that's as big as winning the Super Bowl!

It's good to celebrate where you are while God changes you into the person He ultimately wants you to be.

Your Small Wins Are Significant Wins

In the book of Ezra, the Israelites who had returned from captivity in Babylon had a dream to rebuild the temple in Jerusalem. It was a huge task under very difficult conditions. After much work, they finally finished the foundation. The Scripture says, "When the builders laid the foundation of the temple of the LORD, the priests in their vestments and with trumpets, and the Levites with cymbals, took their places to praise the LORD" (Ezra 3:10 NIV). *Wait...what?* All they had completed was the foundation, yet the project manager called for everyone to stop and celebrate. They didn't have any walls up. No roof. No flooring. I imagine some of the box checkers and high achievers on the crew said, "This was just step one. What are y'all doing?" Some of the others probably thought, *This is going to take forever, and we're going to run out of money and supplies. We'll never finish.* Rather than focusing on the work that was left to be done, they celebrated the good. They were enjoying the process. They were celebrating the progress even though it was unfinished. They were celebrating a partial victory. It wasn't a small win; it was a significant one.

> It's time you called for a celebration over the foundation in your life.

You'll have a hard time living in peace and joy if you only focus on what's incomplete in your life. I encourage you to see that it's time you called for a celebration over the foundation in your life. You may not be where you ultimately want to be, but thank God that you're not where you used to be. In fact, I suggest that you pause from reading and just think about the progress you *have* made and celebrate the good right now.

My wife, Summer, has been battling vertigo for several years. We think it was triggered from a plane ride. She's seen countless doctors and tried various techniques, but she hasn't experienced the complete healing we're believing for yet. It's been a daily mental and physical battle, with some days being better than others, but there isn't a moment she doesn't have to fight it. The vertigo has kept her off of many flights and from traveling to places should would love to see. She has been limited even to the point of not being able to drive long distances because the motion can exacerbate the dizziness. Summer is a go-getter, a hard worker, which makes it an even greater battle.

Recently I was at Lakewood Church preparing for an event with Joel and Victoria Osteen and some of our team. As we were discussing our plans, Victoria received a text message from Summer telling her that she was going to drive and meet up with us. We couldn't believe it, knowing the toll it took for Summer to fight the anxiety of getting into the car to drive. This was more than an hour's drive in bad traffic, full of turns, stops, and other opportunities for the vertigo to increase. Despite knowing what was potentially ahead of her, she did it afraid. When she pulled into the church parking lot, Victoria and I high-fived! We celebrated! As we did, the team around us looked a little confused, as if to say, "What's the big deal? All she did was drive a car?" But they didn't know what it cost Summer to push through the anxiety. Summer walked into the church, and without hesitation, the three of us high-fived, hugged, and celebrated.

What happened? Summer made a free throw. She's not completely healed, but she experienced a partial victory, a small win, and we celebrated it. (By the way, get some friends like Victoria who will celebrate every free throw you make in life and encourage you to keep shooting!)

> As you begin to thank God for where you are and what you do have, He will continue to transform you and take you to new levels.

I want you to know that God is at work in your life, changing and transforming you. The apostle Paul says, "And I am certain that God, who began the good work within you, will *continue his work* until it is finally finished on the day when Christ Jesus returns" (Philippians 1:6 NLT). You are an unfinished work. You may not be completely healed or where you desire to be in a certain area of your life. But as you begin to thank God for where you are and what you do have, He will continue to transform you and take you to new levels.

So feel good about who you are even though you're still struggling in some areas. Thank God for the foundation even though you don't have the walls up. Take time to celebrate when you hit a free throw. The wins may be small, but they are significant. They may not look like your friend's wins. People may not understand why you are celebrating, but they are your wins, and they are significant. I've learned that the more you thank God, the more He'll release strength, healing, favor, and breakthroughs in your life. If you celebrate the progress, God is going to finish what He started in your life. You're going to break bad habits, accomplish dreams, and become everything He's created you to be.

Easy Is Overrated

I'll never forget my son's *second* day of kindergarten.

Denver's first day was great. It was an exciting day as he and my daughter, Haven (who was going into fourth grade), were going to the same school together. Both of them were dressed and ready to go early. We took pictures (signs included), piled in the car, and drove them to school. Later that day, when the bus dropped them off, Haven walked in full of excitement, telling us all about her new teacher and friends.

In stark contrast, Denver walked in much slower, dropped his backpack, and sprawled his whole body out on the hallway floor. He was exhausted and barely gave us any feedback about his day. Fast forward to day two. Haven came downstairs just as excited as she'd been on day one. But as she began to eat breakfast, she said, "D's still in his bed." With only twenty minutes before we needed to leave, I yelled up the stairs for Denver to come down. Moments later, he walked into the kitchen still in his pajamas, wrapped in his comforter, hair all a mess. He sat at the counter and laid his head down.

I said, "Denver, what are you doing? You have to get dressed! You have school today!"

He slowly lifted his head, looked at me through a frown, and exclaimed, "I have to go *again?*"

As Summer and I held back our laughter, Haven looked at him and said, "D, get used to it. This is for the *rest* of your life."

Denver assumed kindergarten was *one* day. In his mind, he had crushed it. He met his teacher, made some new friends, did some easy work, and *bam...done*. Kindergarten was *over.* What he soon came to realize is that Kindergarten takes a year to complete. He learned some things take time. Not everything is done in a day. Growing isn't always *easy*.

> Sometimes the seasons of greatest growth and advancement are the ones that are most difficult.

When it comes to your development and progress, *easy is overrated*. Fun and easy doesn't always mean fruitful. Oftentimes, hard means fruitful. Sometimes the seasons of greatest growth and advancement are the ones that are most difficult. Without them, we will never realize our full potential. We all face things in our life that are difficult and challenging, and too often we get discouraged and give up on our dreams and think that's the end. But God uses these hard seasons as a part of His plan.

I want to encourage you to change your perspective of the hard seasons or what's challenging. Think of your life like a seed that cannot germinate in the light. As long as it's with the other seeds in its packet, relaxed and comfortable, it will never become what it was meant to be. It has to be planted in the soil, in that dark place, so that what's inside can come to life. In a similar way, God uses the hard seasons to bring out the best in you. The seeds of potential can only be released in a dark place. Hard is not our preferred method, but it is necessary for us to reach our full purpose.

Notice some of the difficult life situations in the Bible. God reveals His plan to Moses that He is going to use him to deliver the Israelites from Egyptian slavery, but there is a catch. Pharaoh, the most powerful person in the world, is going to say no. In other words, though this is God's plan, it won't be easy. Or consider that David was equipped only with a rock and a slingshot to defeat a fully armored giant. Really, God? Can we get the man a tank or a fully loaded drone? There are far easier ways to defeat a giant. Then think about Gideon. He starts with 32,000 soldiers to fight a massive enemy army, but God steps in and trims his troops down to 300. What? Why?

> God's way isn't always the easiest, but it's always the best.

God's way isn't always the easiest, but it's always the best. Don't assume because it's hard that you are off track and not called to it. Take hope in the fact that there's deep, significant purpose in what you are facing or going through. The apostle Paul says,

"There is a wide-open door for a great work here, although many oppose me" (1 Corinthians 16:9 NLT). Opposition and opportunity simultaneously confronted Paul in Ephesus. If some things are hard in your life right now, it may not be because you're doing something wrong; it may be because you're doing something right. Paul understood this principle and chose to stay the course and face the opposition, and many lives in the Ephesian church were eternally different because he did.

Be encouraged that the enemy wouldn't oppose you if you didn't have something great in front of you. He doesn't just fight for where you are; he fights for where you are going.

Bounce-Back Power

My kids have always loved bouncy balls (me too). You can find these balls, big and small, lying around our house. Sometimes I hear them being bounced off walls or knocking over picture frames and sometimes getting chewed on by our dog, Harley. The unique thing about these balls is that they are made of an elastic material that allows them to bounce back against hard surfaces. You can't discover the ball's full potential and see what it's made of by bouncing or dropping it on anything soft. But if you throw it against a hard surface, you'll see the bounce-back power that's inside. It's designed to bounce back, not to get stuck or break apart.

I've found that there are always challenges and obstacles that come our way to cause us to stumble and fall or knock us down. Many times the key to progress and becoming all we are created to be simply involves learning to get back up. Proverbs 24:16 says, "A righteous person may fall seven times, but he gets up again" (GW). You can do that because you possess the power inside to bounce back. The Bible says that the same power that raised Jesus from the dead lives inside you (see Romans 8:11). That means you possess the same power that defeated death, Hell, and the grave!

When you get knocked down, you have to realize that you have bounce-back power. Nothing you will face has the power to keep you from getting to your destiny. People can't stop you, situations can't stop you, and the enemy can't stop you. Whether it's a financial setback, a divorce, or a job layoff, you just have to make the decision to exercise the power you possess and bounce back. You can know that God is using the struggle to develop your character and will work all things out for your good. It's not that God causes everything, but He uses everything to bring us out better.

But we have to realize we can't do it by ourselves. We're like little children who get ice cream on their face when eating a cone. Their first instinct is to use the back of their hand to wipe their face clean, pushing the cream across their chin and cheek to their hair. It's only a matter of time before the creamy hand swipes their shirt, and it's a worse mess than when it started. Too often that's what we do when we have things in our life we're not proud of, areas where we've stumbled and fallen. We instinctively try to clean the mess up on our own, but it only leads to a bigger mess.

Children eventually learn a secret. When they get ice cream or chocolate on their face, they lean over to Mom. Have you ever witnessed a mom clean a child's face? It is supernatural. The technique and precision as she dips the napkin in the water and wipes is unbelievable. The job is done with such focus and gentleness until every spot is cleaned. This is what God wants to do with us. He wants to clean, restore, and transform us. He wants to finish the work that He began in you. So where are you leaning or looking to for internal progress? Yourself? Or are you leaning into Jesus, the only One who has the power to change you from the inside out?

> Are you trying to change on your own or through God's power?

How we attempt and go about change in our heart and life is critical. When we fall and stumble, we can try to get up using our own strength, or we can rely on His power inside to help us bounce back. Are you trying to change on your own or through God's power? One way is exhausting and short-lived; the other is liberating and lasting. My encouragement is to change your perspective of lasting growth and development. Look to Jesus and trust His work inside, and you will begin to see things change in your life that you never thought could change.

One day Jesus turned His attention to the religious teachers and Pharisees and said, "For you are so careful to clean the outside of the cup and the dish, but inside you are filthy—full of greed and self-indulgence! You blind Pharisees! First wash the inside of the cup and the dish, and then the outside will become clean, too" (Matthew 23:25–26 NLT). What was the Pharisees' problem? They were leaning the wrong way. They focused all their attention on trying to clean themselves up on the outside with their own strength. Jesus says that His way works from the inside out.

> Living right starts with believing right.

Religion can't penetrate the heart and set you free. We don't have the power to change our hearts. Only God can do that. Permanent change starts on the inside. Living right starts with believing right. Religion says to clean yourself up, then come to

God. Jesus says to come to Him just as you are, and as you allow and invite Him into your life, He will transform you from the inside out.

The Power to Change

When I was in high school, on a Friday night right after I got my driver's license, I took my car out with a friend who was going to sleep over. We were going to hang out at another friend's house. As I left home, my mom gave me a clear rule: Be home before ten o'clock. Well, I sort of lost track of the time and suddenly realized it was midnight. Instead of calling home and letting my parents know we were on the way, I decided to try to sneak in, hoping that we wouldn't wake them up and they'd never know. As I pulled into our driveway, I turned off the lights, put the car into neutral, turned off the engine, and silently coasted quickly toward my parking spot in the pitch-black darkness. All of a sudden we slammed into something that literally flipped the car up on its side and tossed my friend to my side of the car! We scrambled to get out, and to my surprise, we had hit a giant black mulch pile that had been delivered earlier that day. Obviously we couldn't see the mulch pile with the lights off. I was so busted...with mulch everywhere. In that moment, I remember thinking, *What am I doing?* There was no way I was talking my way out of this one. We rolled the car off the pile and went to bed, knowing we were caught. Let's just say I had a lot of yard work and cleanup to do, not only the next day but for the rest of that summer.

Ever had those moments? Moments when you see a gap between who you are and who you know you should be? You don't have to hit a mulch pile to spot it. It's when you react to your spouse harshly. It's when you don't have the funds but you go ahead and buy that thing you want so badly, when you gossip, or when your ego drives you to post something that's out of character.

We all have these moments that reveal the gap between who we are and who we know we should be. We know what we are supposed to do but we don't do it.

The apostle Paul wrote nearly half the books of the New Testament and was an incredible spiritual leader. You would think his life had no gaps, that he had a flawless interior life. But that wasn't the case. He wrote with great transparency: "I do not understand what I do. For what I want to do I do not do, but what I hate I do" (Romans 7:15 NIV).

> Ever had those moments? Moments where you see a gap between who you are and who you know you should be?

I find hope in the fact that Paul didn't hide this gap in his life. He didn't try to fill it in with something else. He didn't try to cover it up or mask it. He didn't say to just try harder or pray harder or try to get rid of the shame by his own willpower. Paul knew that he did not possess the power to change himself internally, that the best he could do was a patchwork, something temporary. There was only one answer for Paul and you and me: "Thanks be to God, who delivers me through Jesus Christ our Lord!" (Romans 7:25 NIV).

Are you attempting to patch issues in your life when Jesus wants to permanently change them? Your responsibility is not to change or put a patch on them, but it is to face the problems, the weaknesses, and the shortcomings. God cannot change you if you are avoiding or ignoring your issues, if you are acting as though you don't have a problem. No, you recognize your weaknesses and at the same time you recognize you can't change yourself, so you simply put yourself in position for God to transform you. Throughout the day, you're praying, "God, I don't want to carry this anger issue, so I'm looking to You and asking You to change me from the inside out." It's declaring throughout your day, "God, I don't want to think these lustful thoughts. I don't want to battle with this addiction anymore, so I'm looking to You and Your power inside to break and remove it." What are you doing? You're taking your eyes off the issues, the failures, and the addiction, and you're fixing your eyes on Jesus. As you change what you focus on, power is released and awakened on the inside and change happens. Those things in your life are lifted off. Sometimes it's instant; sometimes it takes time. In both cases, it's God's power that does the work.

> Are you attempting to patch issues in your life when Jesus wants to permanently change them?

A Work in Progress

When Summer and I began to build our house, it was just a plan on paper and a plot of land. We were excited and just about every day we would drive to the construction site to check out the progress. During one period of the building process, the frame was complete and the roof was in place, but the shingles weren't on yet. A big storm moved in, and for two days it rained on and off. When we went over to check on the house, it was a huge mess. The living room had about three inches of dirty water in it, plywood was floating, and workers had tracked mud throughout the house. Outside, trash was piled high. It looked like a disaster zone, with supplies all out of place.

But we didn't say, "This place is such a mess that it's never going to be what we wanted. Let's stop construction." We knew it was part of the process. To the untrained eye, and from our perspective, the construction site was disorganized and a chaotic mess, but our architect assured us that it was no big deal. He drew up the plans and knew exactly where it was all going and how it was going to come together. He wasn't worried because you can't have a beautiful house without rain, mud, Sheetrock dust, and what looks like disorder.

In the same way, you have to see the things that are messy in your life, the things you struggle with, the things that seem out of place, as simply a part of being under construction. The disappointment, the delay, and the broken relationship are all a part of the process. God is the architect who has designed a specific plan for your life. He is the builder who started a good work in you, and the messy places can't stop your destiny. It may feel and look like you're stuck, but the architect of your life is saying, "You're not a finished product. I'm still working on you, and I'm going to bring you to completion."

> It may feel and look like you're stuck, but the architect of your life is saying, "You're not a finished product. I'm still working on you, and I'm going to bring you to completion."

The enemy will whisper, "Look at the water in your living room. Look at the flaws, the weaknesses, the mistakes." Just remind him, "There's a powerful force inside me that's at work. I may have some messy areas, but God is my builder." The enemy taunts, "You still struggle with your addiction, and you will always have that temper." Just reply, "It may appear that way, but I know I'm under construction on the inside. God's power is eliminating it, and it's only a matter of time before I'm completely free."

There may be times when you think you've made too many mistakes and missed God's plan. But God says, "The plans I have for you…are plans for good and not for evil, to give you a future and a hope" (Jeremiah 29:11 TLB). What God has designed for you does not end in defeat, in mediocrity, in addictions, or in injustice. The apostle Paul says, "God always leads us in triumph in Christ" (2 Corinthians 2:14 NIV). Your story ends in victory. In other words, if there are things that are holding you back, things that are out of place, things that are messy, it just means that the job is not done.

Stop beating yourself up, thinking about how you don't measure up or how you've done too much wrong. No, stir your faith up and remind yourself, "I'm a masterpiece in the making. My God says so."

If you have some chocolate on your face today, lean into the One who can permanently change you. You may have fallen, but keep getting back up in His grace. You are a work in progress with a builder who knows how to bring you to completion.

So go on and live the dream today. You don't have to wait until all your weaknesses or flaws are gone before you can be happy. Change your perspective and learn to enjoy the process, not just endure it. Start celebrating the good on your way to great!

CHAPTER FOUR

DO IT AFRAID

Step into the Miracle

Wh
hen I was in college, two of my friends and I decided to go skydiving. We found a facility just outside downtown Chicago and decided one Saturday we were going to do it. Since none of us had been skydiving before, we had to go through some extensive training prior to the jump at the facility. We arrived early, signed our lives away, got fitted for our jumpsuits, and began walking through the jump instructions. I was so nervous. The more training we received, the realer it got that *I was going to jump out of a perfectly good airplane.* Next thing you know, they paired each of us up with an instructor who would tandem jump with us. My instructor had a bleached blond mohawk and said it

was his day off, but he came in for the fun of it. I wasn't sure if that was to make me feel more at peace or further crawl into my skin. They proceeded to escort us to this small, eight-passenger plane that had all its seats removed. We climbed in, sat on its metal floor tied to our instructors, and took off.

> "Nick, you just gotta *do it afraid.*"

As we climbed to 12,000 feet, I could feel my hands getting sweaty and my heart pounding. When we got to the jump height of 14,000 feet, one of the instructors slid the side door open. The blast of wind hit all of us in the plane.

It...Just...Got...REAL.

The first jumper slowly walked up to the opening with his instructor at his back, looked over the edge of the plane, and they jumped. They dropped so fast, I could barely see them. Then I watched my friend scoot up, get to the edge, and he and his instructor dropped. My other friend stepped up, and in a second, they disappeared. They dropped so fast, I couldn't even hear them scream. Then it was *my* turn. I was terrified as I slowly walked to the ledge of the door. Panicked thoughts were rushing through my mind, such as, *I can't do this! Turn back! I don't remember when I'm supposed to pull the cord! I don't know what gauges to look at!* I reluctantly inched my final steps to the ledge, definitely having second and third thoughts about this jump. Just as I stepped on the ledge, the instructor said something I'll never forget:

"Nick, you just gotta *do it afraid.*"

Before I could reply or even agree, our momentum carried us, and I took the STEP and we DROPPED! It was a sixty-second free fall, with an unbelievable feeling as adrenaline surged through my body as we fell. Then suddenly in the middle of the chaos I felt a tap on my arm from the instructor. He pointed to the gauges on my wrist, then he took my hand and put it on the rip cord release handle. I pulled it, the chute opened, and in an instant everything was quiet and calm. He led my hands to the ropes where I could turn and control the chute. The view of Chicago as we soared through the air was breathtaking. A few minutes later, with his help, we landed safely.

That was one of the most frightening and best experiences of my life. What I will never forget is that this memorable moment all began with a step—not an easy step, a very scary step. I had to do it afraid, in the face of fear. I had to place my trust in the instructor, who would ultimately lead and guide me safely to our destination. I wonder if there are some things in your life right now that God is inviting you into that look a bit frightening. Could there be some new levels and opportunities in front of you, but you're letting fear stop you from pursuing them? Oftentimes we feel compelled to do something or say something, and we know it's the right thing to do, but it's scary. We have a dream of a new house, but it seems too big. We're not qualified for the position at work that we know we can do. The baby you've been hoping for is on the way, but are you ready? Are you allowing fear to keep you from believing and stepping out for that promise? If you wait until all your fear is gone, you might be waiting your whole life. I'm encouraging you to step out and show God your faith in spite of, or in the face of, your fear. *Do it afraid.* When you do, I believe that, as the instructor was for me, God will be with you. He will direct you, give you the grace, the wisdom, and the provision for every step of the way.

Most of us have things in our life that we know we are supposed to be doing. The problem is, we often wait for the "perfect time." The reality is that may never come. King Solomon says, "There are *some* things that you cannot be sure of. You must

> Are you allowing fear to keep you from believing and stepping out for that promise?

take a chance. If you wait for perfect weather, you will never plant your seeds. If you are afraid that every cloud will bring rain, you will never harvest your crops" (Ecclesiastes 11:4 ERV). In other words, if you wait for perfect conditions or when it's convenient to do things in your life, such as when fear isn't present, you will never become or do anything of significance.

Motion Activated

Something crazy happened to me the other day. I needed a few things and was walking to the entrance to our local Target. As I approached the entrance, the big double doors were closed, but I kept walking toward them and suddenly something incredible happened—the doors opened all by themselves! Right before my eyes, they opened. I didn't even have to touch the doors. These two sets of doors somehow knew to open at the perfect time so I could walk in and get everything I needed. It was amazing!

You're probably thinking, *What planet does this guy live on?* Okay, I admit that I am fully aware of the phenomenon of motion-activated doors. But I thought it might help illustrate how God calls us to step forward in faith and do what He is asking us to do. When it comes to God, we have to realize that He has many blessings, relationships, and provisions for us, but they are motion activated. Everything I needed was right inside that Target, and even though there were two closed doors preventing me from entering, it was when I walked toward them that they opened. I wonder how many times we see closed doors around the things God has for us, and instead of walking toward those doors, we turn around and walk away. I wonder how many blessings we have missed out on because we stayed motionless when God was asking us to take a step even though the doors were closed.

> I wonder how many times we see closed doors around the things God has for us, and instead of walking toward those doors, we turn around and walk away.

The psalmist says, "The LORD directs the *steps* of the godly" (Psalm 37:23 NLT). Notice that He doesn't direct your stance; He directs your *step*. You have to give Him your step. As you step, He directs it and establishes it where it needs to be.

When our daughter, Haven, was around four years old and preparing for kindergarten, we wanted to sell our house and move to a different school district so she could attend an elementary school we really loved. We began to pray and ask God to direct us and open a door. We started looking at homes in neighborhoods around the school and quickly realized that selling our house at a price high enough to afford the more expensive houses in this new school zone would require a miracle. So we did what we knew to do and surrendered our situation to God.

Then one day I came home from work, and as I pulled into the garage, I saw a stack of flattened cardboard boxes. I thought it was odd, but I did what I normally do with recyclables and put them in the recycle bin. This continued to happen for a few days. I would come home, see the random boxes, and move them into the bin. Then one day I came home and there was the largest stack of boxes yet. I went into the house and asked Summer why there were boxes stacked in the garage. At the time, she was a full-time dental hygienist and would usually beat me home every day.

Summer said, "Oh, I brought those boxes home from work. I figured we would need empty boxes for packing our things *when* we move."

Yup. Here my wife was trying to save boxes in faith, and I was throwing them away! I was stunned. That challenged my faith. She was preparing for something we were believing for. I was asking in faith, but Summer went a step further and showed God her faith. If you will move, even just a lit- tle, God will do a miracle! Months later, those boxes were filled with our stuff, because we sold our house for what we were asking, and we found a brand-new home in the school district we were believing for!

> If you will move, even just a little, God will do a miracle!

God is motion activated. He's looking to bless your steps. It didn't make sense for Summer to ask her coworkers for empty boxes, but in faith, she did it anyway. It can be scary taking steps toward something that God has put in your heart to do. Stir your faith today. If you will move, even just a little, God will do a mir- acle! It's time to step into favor, freedom, and the promises God has for you.

Take the Step

My friends J. D. and Alini had been married for nine years, and due to a wide range of complex circumstances, they weren't able to get pregnant. They were in a very busy season with their jobs, liv- ing in a small apartment, still trying to finish school, and seeking financial stability. Yet they had a dream to have a child. Then one night, after hearing a message about taking a step of faith, Alini did just that. She went to a baby store and bought a small baby rattle. Despite the fear of the unknown, despite their circumstances, she bought something to show God their faith and remind them of the dream and promise they were believing for. They told me that purchase was a turning point. With God's guidance, everything fell into place. A few weeks later, they were expecting! A few months later, they were miraculously able to buy their first home. As a generous bonus, they were given three months' maternity and paternity leave with full pay. They not only had a healthy baby girl who would play with that rattle, but they were able to bring her to a beautiful home that God had provided for them. Buying a baby rattle was the step they felt they needed to take. It felt weird, and it didn't make sense, given their financial situation, but they did it anyway. Oh, and by the way, they have four kids now!

It's time to take a step. It's time to do what God has been prompting you to do! When you make a move in spite of the fear of the unknown, He will move and do the impossible.

In John 6, thousands of people who had seen Jesus heal the sick had followed Him to a hill by the Sea of Galilee where He was with His disciples. As they approached, Jesus asked Philip where they could buy bread to feed them. Philip didn't have a clue, but Andrew mentioned there was a young boy there who had two small fish and five loaves of bread. Now use your holy imagination with me here. These men approached a kid and asked for his lunch. It's easy to assume this kid cheerfully obliged, but I had a ten-year-old son who has practically fought his sister over his chicken strip meal from Chick-fil-A. I'm just saying that this may not have happened as smoothly as we think. This unnamed boy was apparently the one person who actually had food that day, but he was being asked to give it up. Say what you want, but I think this kid was the one who exercised the most faith that day. He was the real hero. He had his food, yet he chose to give it, to release it. He trusted the disciples and Jesus enough to hand over his mom's nicely packed lunch, so Jesus could work a miracle with it. The kid took a step, and Jesus did a miracle with it.

> I wonder what God has planned to do with your lunch. With your seemingly small step of obedience.

What's interesting is that Jesus could have made food appear out of nowhere. God could have flown in some chicken, better yet some Whataburger (my Texas family will understand). Instead, He chose to use the lunch, or should I say, the step, of a boy. When the boy gave his lunch, Jesus didn't assess the lunch and conclude that it was too small. He didn't send it back to the boy, deeming it unusable. No, He took what was small in man's eyes and did the miraculous with it. I wonder what God has planned to do with your lunch. With your seemingly small step of obedience. I wonder what doors of opportunity He's going to open, what business He's going to bless, what miracle He's going to deliver because you took a step and showed Him your faith.

Dig a Ditch

In 2 Kings 3, the armies of Israel, Judah, and Edom had joined together against the Moabites, but found themselves in what seemed like a hopeless predicament. After seven days, their route through the Desert of Edom left them with no water for themselves or their animals. One of the king's officers suggested they ask the prophet Elisha for counsel. They approached him for a word from God, and Elisha told them to do something that didn't make sense. He said, "Dig ditches all over the valley. Here's what will happen. You won't hear the wind, and you won't see the rain, but this valley is going to fill up with water, and your army and your animals will drink their fill. This is easy for God to do. He will also hand over Moab to you." So the people did what Elisha told them to do. They grabbed their shovels and began digging ditches all over the valley. Can you imagine how foolish they had to feel while digging ditches? Can you imagine the conversations as they dug? "Why are we doing this? There's never been water here, and there's no sign of it coming. We're wasting our time. We should be sharpening our swords and preparing for battle, not digging ditches."

Well, the next morning when they woke up, water was pouring into the valley from the west like a flash flood. Everything God spoke through Elisha happened. God provided for them. He did the miracle He promised. But notice what preceded it. He told them to dig ditches all over the valley. In other words, "Take a step, make a move, exercise your faith, and when you do, I

> Instead of wondering how it's going to happen and allowing fear to hold you back, it's time to dig a ditch.

will fulfill My promise and do what only I can do." What you are believing God to do in your life is an easy thing for Him to do. Instead of wondering how it's going to happen and allowing fear to hold you back, it's time to dig a ditch.

It's time to apply for that next job.

It's time to break ground for that new business.

It's time to buy the air freshener for that new car.

It's time to collect and stack some boxes.

It's time to buy the welcome mat for the new house.

It's time to get a suit jacket for that promotion.

It's time to get the rattle for your new baby.

Set a New Standard

In January 1967, my wife's grandfather, Pastor Eugene Whitcomb, had a vision and a dream. He went to Rockford, Illinois, to pastor the First Assembly of God Church. At the time the Sunday service was averaging sixty to eighty people in a small building in downtown Rockford. Pastor Eugene had a vision to see more people in that area impacted. The church owned a piece of property that was seven acres, but he was convinced it wasn't big enough for what God wanted to do. Critics tried to talk him out of believing for more, and experts in his own association said it was foolish to look for anything bigger. Despite the naysayers, he would drive around the outskirts of the city looking for property. One day he found thirty-two acres of land that were in the middle of cornfields. They weren't for sale, but he believed that was where they were supposed to build. He would drive out there, walk around the field, and pray. Feeling stronger with each visit that it was the land they were supposed to buy, he contacted the farm owner several times and made multiple offers, but the farmer refused to sell. At one point the farmer said there was a group in Chicago that wanted to buy it for substantially more than Eugene offered.

In the face of doubt, fear, and many rejections, Eugene was persistent. One night around midnight, he received a call from the farm owner, who was extremely angry with the way the Chicago business was dealing with him. He said he would sell the land to Eugene for a cheaper price if they met first thing in the morning and sealed the deal. That night, Eugene called all the church board members together to meet and get the papers signed. They did, and the deal was done. It was a miracle! God provided the land for half of what it was worth.

Eugene started designing the plans for a 1,500-seat church. Everyone thought he was crazy and said it was way too big, given the current size of the congregation. There were some megachurches at the time, but this would be one of the largest Assemblies of God churches in America. Eugene oversaw the building project, and by 1974, not only was the church building finished and full every Sunday, but they also completed the construction of a kindergarten-through-eighth-grade Christian school next to the church. The church and school were giving hope to families every week from all over the region. In the face of fear and opposition, he took a step and his dream became a reality.

Eugene was also a pilot and owned a twin-engine airplane. He used it primarily to fly to and from mission projects all over the country. Just after the school was completed and open, Eugene flew five men on a mission trip to South Dakota to complete another school. This time the Bible school they had been building was on an Indian reservation. When it was completed, they departed for their trip back. However, just an hour into the flight, the plane had a mechanical failure and went down. There were no survivors. Eugene was only forty-one years old. However, even though he died, his dream and legacy live on. The church he started in the middle of the cornfields became a beacon of hope to thousands in the Rockford area. The school he had a vision to start would develop and be instrumental in shaping my wife's faith and education, along with thousands of others. In the summer of 1998, that church's youth ministry held its annual summer camp in Spencer Lake, Wisconsin. I was invited to that camp by a friend and gave my life to Jesus, as mentioned in chapter 2. Soon after, I met Summer. The rest is history.

What's my point? You never know what impact your step will have. It doesn't just affect you; it affects those coming behind you. Imagine if Eugene had listened to the naysayers. Imagine if he had allowed fear to keep him in his comfort zone. Imagine if he didn't step out or waited for conditions to be perfect. Many lives, including my own, would look drastically different today.

> Your step, as insignificant as it may feel or seem in the moment, has the potential to change the trajectory of not only your life, but the lives of many around you.

Your step, as insignificant as it may feel or seem in the moment, has the potential to change the trajectory of not only your life, but the lives of many around you. Never underestimate the power of one step!

Choose to Stand

In 2 Samuel 23, we read about King David's "mighty men." These were the warriors whom David chose to bring close to him. These were the ones whom he chose to move forward with him. These were the ones whom he wanted to lead and fight beside him. One of the mighty men was named Shammah. Verses 11–12 describe a moment that tells us a lot about who Shammah was and the type of people whom David wanted around him. The Philistines had gathered to attack the Israelite army, which was clearly not ready for war. The Philistines were Goliath's people, warriors by nature. When the Israelites saw the Philistines gathered in a field of lentils, they fled. I'm sure the Philistines felt pretty good about winning the battle without even having to fight.

But the Bible distinguishes one man from the pack. Shammah

stood his ground against them, alone, in the middle of that field. Perhaps the Philistines sent a few men initially to take care of him, then more, and more. Their attempts failed, and the Philistines quickly realized that this army of one was a problem. They sent team after team to destroy him, but Shammah fought the Philistines back, and the Lord brought the victory. The Philistines retreated, and Shammah, exhausted, tired, and wounded,

> This man did by himself what the Israelites didn't believe they could do together.

returned to his people. He probably didn't say a word. His presence was probably enough as he walked into the camp to say, "I'm here. I stayed, and I *stood*, and God did it." Can you imagine the feelings of the other Israelite soldiers? Embarrassed. Jealous. Ashamed. They ran in fear, yet he stayed. This man did by himself what the Israelites didn't believe they could do together. God did through him what He longed to do through them all.

It's easy to allow fear to keep you on the run. Showing God your faith can be hard at times. It's often not a place of comfort. But as with Shammah, it is a place of victory. It is a place where you live and fight for what's in you. And you can discover that it changes the game for those who are living on the run around you. Imagine the Israelites around the campfire trying to explain that the only option they had was to run, until one innocent child asked, "Well, where's Shammah?" You may have had parents or grandparents who chose to run. You may have grown up around people who settled for mediocrity, who compromised their dreams and purpose in the face of fear of the unknown or what others might say. Today, you can set a new standard. As Shammah did, you can choose to stand. You may feel alone, but God is with you. He is not only going to fight for you, but He's going to use your step to influence many others around you to stand for what they are believing for as well.

I think of my friend Brett, who grew up in Philadelphia. He loved basketball, but he didn't play at a high level. He had a dream to coach in the NBA, but many people told him he couldn't because he didn't have the playing experience. Well, it's hard to say you can't reach your dream because you don't know the right people or have the experience when Brett has been an assistant coach in the NBA, having coached All-Stars and MVPs at the highest level.

Then there's my friend Julio, who came to the United States when he was nineteen years old. He was a dishwasher who had a dream to own his own restaurant. It's hard to say you can't own a business because you don't come from the right family or neighborhood when a guy such as Julio is now a successful owner of not just one, but multiple restaurants.

> Your step of faith can give others the permission to step as well.

I recently read about Roger Bannister. He was the first man to run the mile in under four minutes. Prior to his record, no one thought the four-minute mark could be broken. Experts said it was impossible. In May 1954, Bannister ran a time of 3 minutes, 59.4 seconds. Here's what's powerful. His record only stood for forty-six days. Once he broke the four-minute barrier, it gave many other runners the hope and belief that it was possible. Today, it is the standard of male professional, middle-distance runners. What once seemed impossible is now the standard. What am I saying? Sometimes God needs you to go somewhere so that you can take others there as well. Your step of faith can give others the permission to step as well.

Don't Put It Off

My first car was a gray 1986 Honda Prelude. I loved that car. It had a sunroof and a CD player (something that spins these small discs and plays music...never mind). You could find me cruisin' on a Saturday, windows down, music blasting out of my 6-by-9 speakers, with NILSON 2 on the license plates. I felt ten feet tall driving that car. However, about six months after we bought it, I started to hear something squeaking every time I pushed the brakes. Instead of getting the brakes looked at or even telling my parents about it, I just ignored the issue and kept driving it. The sound from the brakes became so constant that it almost became normal to me. I got so used to ignoring the sound or playing my music so loud that I didn't even recognize it anymore. Then one day about ten months later, I pulled into the school parking lot to get ready for one of my first fall football practices. I went straight into a parking space that was directly in front of the field where all the band members and cheerleaders were practicing. I pressed the brake, and the pedal went straight to the floorboard! The car didn't slow down, jumped the curb, and rolled

> I wonder what God has been whispering to you about that you've been putting off or ignoring.

right onto the practice field. The whole band stopped and looked through the cloud of dirt to discover NILSON 2 needing some assistance. All of my friends, teammates, and the cheerleaders fell on the ground laughing. It was embarrassing, to say the least.

The car was towed to a local mechanic, who asked me, "How long have you been hearing the brakes squeak?" It had been so long that I didn't remember. Without giving me time to guess, he proceeded to say, "Well, what *was* a hundred-dollar problem has now become a thousand-dollar problem." I had ignored the sounds and signs of a problem, thinking that if I avoided it, it would just go away. Obviously, it only got worse.

I wonder what God has been whispering to you about that you've been putting off or ignoring.

"Break up with him. It's toxic for you."

"Step up and serve."

"Forgive."

"You need to rest more."

"Take a break from social media."

Often we avoid doing things, not because we don't know how but because we are afraid of what might be on the other end of our step. It's not that God wants to take something from you. It's the opposite. He's wanting to protect you, and in the process He's getting something *to* you. It's so important to remember that we walk by faith and not by sight. When you can't see even two steps ahead, it takes immense courage and strength to take the next step. It can be easier to go back or to stand still. Moving forward is never easy. There's always resistance. There's always uncertainty. There are always obstacles. You will have to trust God even when you can't trace Him.

> You will have to trust God even when you can't trace Him.

You'll have to believe that He is good and does good even when nothing feels or looks good. I want to encourage you to step out and do it afraid. If you've prayed, planned, and are as prepared as you can possibly be, then it's time to step out in faith to find out if it's really God leading you. Don't panic. God is big enough to get you back on track if you happen to misstep. No one gets it right the first time every time. I certainly don't.

Jeremiah 1:12 says that God watches over His Word, anxious to perform it. God is eager to be good to you and move mountains in your life. But what moves God is not your need. What moves God is your faith and trust in Him. I believe and declare that as you show God your faith and take a step, God is going to move and set miracles in motion and perform His Word in your life. You are

> Stop waiting for fear to diminish or for the conditions to be just right in order to move toward your purpose and promise. Take that step into your destiny and start livin' the dream!

going to see doors of opportunity open and see His goodness and favor show up in your life as never before. Get a new perspective on your first step today. That step may appear small to you and maybe to others. But your step of obedience has the potential to have a lasting impact not only in your life, but in generations to come. Stop waiting for fear to diminish or for the conditions to be just right in order to move toward your purpose and promise. Take that step into your destiny and start livin' the dream!

CHAPTER FIVE

GOD TREES

Discover Your Prepared Blessings

One hot Houston afternoon, Summer and I went boating with some friends. After several hours on the lake, a few of us needed to go ashore and run and get food. Sum and the rest of the crew were going to stay on the boat until I returned. The boat pulled up to the pier, and I stepped onto the dock. As I pushed the boat away from the dock, I realized that my car keys were still on the boat, which was now drifting away. I yelled for Summer to throw me the keys. She picked them up, wound up like a pitcher, and launched them to me. I watched in what seemed like slow motion as my keys flew inches over my outstretched hand, bounced on the dock, and splashed into the water. My heart sank as my keys disappeared into the murky water. I was stunned. My house keys, car keys, and work keys were all gone. No spares. Lost at the bottom of the lake. I didn't know what to do.

Before I could even begin to plan how I was going to start searching, a couple seemed to appear out of nowhere and walked over and offered to help. They had been on the other end of the pier and saw what happened. But this couple weren't there to go boating for the day or take a dip in the lake. No, they were holding long ropes with thick circle magnets on the ends. It was a bit bizarre. They walked over to where the keys had fallen in and tossed their ropes into the water. After a few minutes, one of the magnets connected to my keys and they pulled them up. I couldn't believe it! It was a miracle!! I thanked them over and over for taking time to help me.

> Whatever problem you are facing, God has already arranged a solution for it.

Here's what's crazy. They had come to the lake that day with ropes and magnets to find lost valuables on the bottom of the lake. I'd never seen people use this method to hunt for valuables in any lake. And they just happened to be there at the exact moment I lost my keys. I choose to believe they were my miracle long before I had a problem. In life, I choose to believe that even if I miss it and get off track, when I choose to stay in faith, God has a solution for me. God has a solution long before we have a problem.

What's sinking in your life? Your finances? Your marriage? A child who's off course? Can I encourage you? Whatever problem you are facing, God has already arranged a solution for it. He's not surprised. He's already prepared what you need—the relationship, the idea, the opportunity—long before you have the problem. Trust Him today. Rest in the promise that none of the things you are going through is taking Him by surprise.

God Has a Tree for You

In Luke 19, we are introduced to a wealthy tax collector named Zacchaeus. He was rich and powerful, but he also was short in stature. Zacchaeus was conflicted in this moment. "He wanted to see who Jesus was, but because he was short he could not see over the crowd" (v. 3 NIV). What could he do about it? He was used to being able to purchase most solutions to his problems, but this problem couldn't be solved with money. The reality is that we all come up short in areas of our lives. You could say we all have a "but." "I can make money, *but* I can't manage it. I can start a relationship, *but* I can't keep one. I can cast a vision, *but* I can't manage one. My business is growing, *but* I'm overwhelmed with anxiety. I have a nice car, *but*… I have my diploma, *but*… I got verified, *but*…" Everybody, and I mean everybody, has a "but"—an area in our life where we come up short.

Zacchaeus didn't come to Jesus because he had power and he was successful. He came to Jesus this way because he had a "but." It wasn't the thing that was working for him; it was the thing that was working against him. Zacchaeus couldn't do anything about it. He had to look beyond himself.

There's always something in our life that we wrestle with, something that pushes us to look beyond ourselves and depend on God. This is where Zacchaeus was. He knew Jesus was coming, and to see Him, he got in His path. Notice that he didn't ask Jesus to get in his path. He found out where Jesus was going and got in His path. It's easy to get consumed with God blessing our agenda and plan, which is good in its place, but the reality is that God has a plan and purpose for your life. Our prayer should be: "God, I want Your will, not mine. Shift my heart and give me the desire to obey and follow You. God, keep me in Your will and on Your path. Lead me and guide me."

Many people in the Bible who needed a miracle prayed these types of prayers and got in God's path. The woman with the issue of blood in Mark 5 got in God's path. Blind Bartimaeus received his sight because he got in God's path. Ten lepers got in the path of Jesus and experienced a miracle. When you get in God's path, and you trust Him, you better believe there will be something waiting for you! This is what happened to Zacchaeus. He thought, *If I just get in His path, everything else will take care of itself.* So he ran down the road ahead of Jesus and saw... a tree.

When you come up short, God will always have a tree for you. Are you coming up short as a husband? As a wife? At work? In your finances? I want you to know that God has a tree divinely placed for you to make up the difference. I've come up short as a friend, father, and leader, but every time God arranged a tree for me. I'm joining my faith with you that this is your time to discover a tree. God has blessings, miracles, and divine relationships to make up the difference between your limitations and your opportunities. You may have a poor track record, but God has a tree. You may have been on drugs, but God has a tree. You may have had a baby out of wedlock, but God has a tree. You may lack education, but God has a tree.

What's interesting about Zacchaeus's story is that trees take a long time to grow. The sycamore tree that Zacchaeus climbed had been there a long time, probably long before his momma and daddy ever laid eyes on each other. God knew long before Zacchaeus was born that he would come up short, and He planted that tree for him. It's amazing to think that God would love you so much and has strategically planned your life and purpose with such precision that He's planted these trees of blessings throughout your life—business partners, friends, a measure of sudden favor, surprise blessings stored up for you. What are these? GOD TREES.

> God knew long before Zacchaeus was born that he would come up short, and He planted that tree for him.

God Trees

In 2007, Summer and I and our three-month-old daughter, Haven, packed up and moved to Houston from Chicago. I was attempting to follow God's plan by taking a job at Lakewood Church. We were excited and honored to come to serve this incredible city and church and the people who make it great. It was such a huge opportunity, but this step of obedience meant moving across the country, away from our family, close friends, and comfort zones. It was hard adjusting, and we had little help balancing church and family, especially when our second child was born.

Soon after Denver was born, we moved into the house we're in now, and when we did, our neighbor came over to introduce himself. His name is Greg. He and his wife had retired from the military and were enjoying an empty nest. Over the next few weeks and months, I noticed Greg doing things for us—pulling in our garbage cans, texting to let me know our garage door was left open, lending his truck to help me with projects, even bringing over unbelievable BBQ that he smoked on his grill. A few years later, I started calling him "The General," because he often stands in his driveway keeping watch for unusual activity on our street. Over the years, Greg is no longer just our neighbor; he's become like family. One day I realized what Greg is to us: A God-planted tree. A tremendous blessing. God called us to something, and He knew long ago what we would need, and He prepared for it. Today, you may be stepping into a new city or job, and you feel that you're unprepared or that you don't have what it takes. Be encouraged, because God has planted trees for you. There will be people who are divinely planted to help mentor, lead, and sustain you in this next chapter of your life.

> God has planted trees for you.

In the book of Exodus, we see God's plan to deliver the Israelites out of Egyptian captivity come to fruition. He calls a man named Moses to be their leader. Moses' upbringing made him a great candidate for this. He possessed a deep sense of justice and would stand up for what was right no matter what the consequences. He had gifts, talents, and leadership skills, but in Exodus 4, we find out that he had a speech impediment. Moses had a "but," a weakness. He was a leader who had come up short. But this didn't take God by surprise. He had chosen Moses for such a task. He hadn't set Moses up to fail; no, He'd arranged a tree for him. As Moses settled into his leadership, God brought his brother, Aaron, alongside him to help communicate directives and messages to the people. Aaron's heart was to serve Moses and his vision. Moses had the plan, and God planted Aaron on Moses' team to communicate it. Together, they fulfilled God's purposes.

Maybe you just ventured forth to start a new business and

you're feeling as though you're coming up short in key areas. God has some key people and ideas already in store for you. Your job is to continue to step out in faith and trust that God is going to provide all that you need at the right time. He can open doors that no man can open or shut. He has divine appointments coming to meet you. God has trees, such as Greg and Aaron, already lined up in your life to help you reach your destiny. He has people and things to strategically make up for your deficiencies. In areas where you are weak, they are strong. God has not called you or asked you to do things for which He hasn't already supplied trees.

Divine Appointments

Fifteen years ago, I walked into a popular hair salon at the mall near our house and was assigned to Bernice. We discussed how I wanted my hair cut and engaged in some small talk throughout the appointment. When she was done, my haircut was *perfect*. There's nothing like the feeling of a fresh haircut. Once you find someone who cuts your hair how you like it, you can't change. Bernice is still cutting not only my hair but Denver's as well. When she started cutting my hair, she only had a few clients; now she's one of the top stylists in the company.

The other day when Bernice was cutting my hair, she reminded me how her clientele grew. She started at the lowest level of the salon when she was twenty-one years old. On her first day on the job, a coworker was running way behind schedule and her next client was in a rush to get her hair styled with a blow dry before a business presentation. So the salon manager put the client in Bernice's chair. Bernice just knew her name and that she was in a hurry for a blow dry. When Connie sat in the chair, she told Bernice about her important business meeting and asked, "If you were my hairdresser and cut my hair, what would you do?"

Bernice looked at her face and hair, thought about it, and gave her a suggestion. Connie loved the idea and said to go ahead if she could do it quickly. Bernice hurried, cut, and styled her hair. As Bernice was finishing up, Connie's husband walked into the salon,

> God is going to bring the right people into your life at the right time.

saw her, and said, "WOW! Your hair looks *amazing*!" Of course, this made Connie's day. She thanked Bernice for squeezing her in and went to pay at the front desk. At the desk, she noticed she was only charged half her usual amount. She went back in and asked Bernice why. Bernice told her that she was a level 1 stylist, and that was her normal price versus her coworker, who was at the highest level. The lady looked at her and said, "You won't be at this level for long. I'm coming back to you, and I'm going to tell all my business partners and friends about you." Within weeks, Bernice had more clients than she could handle. Within a few months, she had fifty long-standing customers and outperformed all the other stylists, receiving one promotion after another. Today, she traces her current success in the company back to that one client.

One connection. One divine appointment catapulted Bernice. She had no idea that Connie was going to show up that day, let alone see things unfold the way they did. What was Connie? A God tree. A divine appointment that changed Bernice's career. You need to stir your faith and believe that, as He did for Bernice, God is going to bring the right people into your life at the right time. He has ordered your steps, and He's also ordered the steps of those He will use to help you get to where you need to be.

Put Yourself in Position

Let's go back to Luke 19 and revisit Zacchaeus. The chief of all the tax collectors, the CEO, the boss, climbs a tree. Stop and think about this for a moment. When was the last time you saw an uber-rich person climb a tree? Like never? Zacchaeus clearly didn't care what people thought about him in that moment. With his title and position and power, he ran and climbed up the tree. In other words, he humbled himself. He had done so many dignified things in his life, but here he wanted to see God so badly that he climbed a tree like a child. Note that Jesus wasn't even there yet. Imagine the people gawking and saying, "Why is that dude running? He looks crazy, climbing a tree." He didn't care what they thought. He thought and believed, *I am in God's path, and this tree is for me. So I can no longer use my shortness as an excuse, because God has provided a tree to make up the difference.*

Jesus reached the spot, looked up and saw Zacchaeus in the tree, and said, "Zacchaeus, come down immediately. I'm going to be a guest in your house today." Zacchaeus came down and they began to walk to his house, which was probably a beautiful house because he was very rich. The crowd immediately began to question Jesus. Social media started to blow up. "Jesus is hanging with Zacchaeus. What's He doing with him? Oh, so is Zacchaeus a Christian now?" They were posting about all the past things Zacchaeus did wrong, all the times he had extorted money from them, but they didn't see the position of his heart that day, which was revealed in the running, the climbing, the waiting.

God uses Zacchaeus to teach us an important key to experiencing these divine trees and reaching our full potential. Fighting to maintain a position of humility, Zacchaeus humbled himself for an inevitable encounter with God. Notice that Jesus came to

Zacchaeus; Zacchaeus didn't come to Jesus. Jesus came to him because he positioned himself not just physically in Jesus' path but in his heart. See, God looks at the position of your heart, and He's looking for a heart of humility. Don't let other opinions, drama, and pride distract you from your position of humility. The enemy

> God looks at the position of your heart, and He's looking for a heart of humility.

can't stop you, so he will try to distract you and get you out of this position. He will lie to you, saying things such as, "Do you realize how foolish you will look? Don't admit the areas where you come up short. There's no recovery from that." Either you can buy into the lie that your shortcomings and weaknesses disqualify you and give up, or you can humble yourself and believe the truth of God's Word, that His power is made perfect in your weakness and He has already provided for your limitations.

Today, it's time to get back on God's path. There's no time for more excuses. Shake off the shame. You don't have to make your own path; God has a path for you. Have you made mistakes? We all have. There's still a path for you. We all have "buts," but there are also God's divinely planted trees in front of each of us.

Shift your perspective of your shortcomings. Choose to believe that those things aren't hindering your destiny, but they are simply pointing you to trees that God has planted to make up the difference in your life. Despite how short you are coming up today, you can *live the dream*, knowing that God has the solution long before you have the problem.

CHAPTER SIX

DREAM TEAM

You Can't Get There Alone

I saw a poll the other day that said the most watched TV show on Netflix was *The Office*, edging out *Friends* by a small percentage. I find this very interesting. Beyond hilarious characters such as Michael Scott and the mystery as to whether Rachel and Ross are going to get together for good, at the core of these shows is a group or a "tribe," you could say. These shows are centered around a group of people who bond, share struggles, and make memories. Over time, they connect deeply, and the reason we love and follow these shows is because there's a huge part of all of us that longs for that type of connection with others. I'd go even further and say that we were designed to need it. We need people around us who can complement, encourage, care for, and bring the best out of us. Key relationships are meant to inspire and challenge you and help you see life from a different perspective. It's vitally important to have the right people in your life. I believe that every dream needs a team. You can't become all you were created to be without the right people in your life.

> Some people say that God is all you need, but is that true?

In Genesis 2, before God created Eve, what did Adam need? Did he have any needs? He was in Eden with God. The place was perfect and beautiful. In paradise, did Adam have any needs? Some people say that God is all you need, but is that true? In paradise, we discover that Adam had other needs besides God. I know, that sounds crazy, but hang with me.

In Genesis 1, we see all that God created for five days, calling each day "good." Then He creates mankind in His own image on the sixth day and says, "Now that's very good." But jump to Genesis 2:18, and He says something is "not good." He says, "It is not good for man to be alone." This wasn't Adam saying, "God, this isn't good for me." This was God telling Adam what he's missing. "Adam, you don't even know it, but you need something else." Adam is in paradise with God, yet it's still not good! Do you see the magnitude of this? "Adam, you need a suitable helper." So God put him to sleep and wakes him up to a relationship with another human whom he didn't know he needed.

I wonder how many of us today are busy doing things for God, running through our lives, but missing out on one need that is critical for us to reach our full potential. As we see with Adam, your destiny, or should I say dream, requires a team. You need some important, healthy relationships. No one gets to their dream by themselves. Here's the good news: On the road map of your life, God has planted divine relationships that will help you reach your destiny and full potential. These relationships are not designed to help you carry out your purpose. They are designed to complement you.

One of the most powerful examples of this was when Jesus was sentenced to a criminal's death on the cross. Jesus didn't have to do this. God could have sent the angel armies to instantly intervene. Jesus had walked on water and spoken the word and calmed raging storms, so escaping soldiers would have been an easy task. He chose to lay His life down for the sins of mankind. He was purposed to stand in the gap for you and for me. They mocked, whipped, and beat Him, then put a cross on His back to carry up the hill of Golgotha. When Jesus hit a point where He physically could not carry the cross any farther, the Roman soldiers forced a man named Simon of Cyrene to carry the cross behind Jesus to the top of the hill where Jesus would be nailed to it and die. The inclusion of Simon is so interesting to me. Think about the fact that Jesus needed someone to help Him carry the cross. Jesus needed Simon to help Him carry out His purpose. So if Jesus needed help fulfilling His purpose, how much more do you and I help? God has lined up people to help you fulfill your destiny. You don't have to do life all by yourself. You don't have to be strong enough all the time. As with Jesus, there will be seasons in your life when you will need the help and support of others. You weren't designed to complete your purpose alone.

Let me put this another way. Life doesn't work until we work it together. Some people may say, "Nick, it's just me and God. I don't need people." I get it. It might look easier to try to navigate life alone and avoid other people with all their needs, the conflicts, and the drama. In many ways, going at it alone can be our default setting because it feels comfortable. But there is no spiritual journey that God will take you on that will disconnect you from humanity and relationships. If you are drawing close to God, you will draw close to the humanity that God created and loves. We need more than God because we were created by God to need one another. Even if conditions are perfect, you still have a need for other people in your life.

> Life doesn't work until we work it together.

Relationships may be messy and difficult to navigate at times, but there's a better option than going through life alone, and it's seeking out others to do life with. Adam needed Eve, and Eve needed Adam. They had each other to confide in, to be open with, and to share their struggles with. We need people who will celebrate, encourage, and complement us. I believe your destiny requires this, and that the danger of isolation is much greater than the risk of vulnerability.

Quality over Quantity

On the other hand, there are many people who have many relationships. You may come from a large family, be a part of a large fraternity, have numerous coworkers whom you consider great friends, or have dozens of acquaintances at church with whom you feel a connection. You have your Saturday golf buddies. We're all "connected" more than ever, and we have spaces and platforms that put us in proximity to people. But I'm not talking about the quantity of your connections; I'm talking about the quality of them. We may have more "friends" than we've ever had, but what we really need to assess is the quality of our relationships because it determines whether the quality of the environment in which we live is healthy.

I think it's interesting that so much emphasis nowadays is put on the environment in which animals are raised, yet we tend to overlook it in our own lives. It doesn't take a scientist to prove that animals raised in overcrowded, dirty, confined spaces are put at high risk of various health problems. For instance, I recently read a fascinating article about the reason that you'll never see a great white shark in an aquarium. While many zoos have tried over and over to house these sharks, the largest of the predatory sharks in the ocean today, within their aquarium walls, most of them die within a few days or weeks no matter what the zookeepers do. There's nothing wrong with the sharks; the problem is in the environment in which they are placed.

> The environment within which you choose to place yourself matters.

You have to know that the environment within which you choose to place yourself matters. Granted, there are some environments you can't control, such as whom you have to share a cubicle with at work. Some things you can't control. I'm talking about the relationships and environments that you can choose. I'm talking about who you are choosing to spend your time with. And I'm not talking about the quantity but rather the quality of your relationships.

Consider an acorn. It's a seed that is full of great potential. It's been designed to become a majestic oak tree. It's healthy, it's strong, but the potential of the seed remains locked inside and it can't grow into all it has been designed to become unless it's planted and rooted in good, nutrient-rich soil, a healthy environment. Hundreds of other potential mighty oak trees are in these acorns, but if one is planted in soil that's full of rocks, thorns, and weeds, it's not going to thrive and produce all it was designed to be. It may survive, but it's not going to be healthy. The problem is not with the seed; it's with the soil.

In Matthew 13, Jesus told a parable about a farmer who planted seeds. The seeds that he planted in good ground grew and produced a flourishing crop. But some of the other seeds fell on rocky ground, and therefore over time didn't produce much. Other seeds fell next to weeds and thorns, which over time hindered the seed from growing. Some seeds fell on the hardened pathway and were consumed by birds. The seeds were of the same quality, each packed with purpose. The difference? The soil. It was the condition and quality of the environment in which the seeds were planted.

It's the same principle with your life. You are a seed. You are full of potential, gifts, and purpose. But if you plant yourself in an unhealthy environment, where the relationships you choose to surround yourself with are filled with compromise, negativity, and limited mind-sets, telling you what you can't accomplish, then you won't see the growth that you have been designed to experience. It's not because there's something wrong with you. You're made in the image of God, and you've been made to bear much fruit. The problem is that you haven't planted yourself in good soil. The thorns, the weeds, and the rocks are limiting your life.

Assess Your Environment

Who you have chosen to surround yourself with, the environment you decide to plant yourself in, has the potential to limit you or unlock you. It's time to assess your soil. We often talk about the importance of self-development, which first begins with your soil development. That means by assessing your environments and relationships. It means being selective with whom and to whom you give your time, energy, and attention. Your potential and dreams are real, but they may not be able to be realized in the limited environment you are in right now. The thorns may be some friends who keep causing you to compromise and choking your growth. The weeds may be the coworkers you hang around, the ones who gossip and talk about how bad life is, always negative, complaining, and criticizing the boss. The rocks may be relatives who tell you why you'll never be successful or never break an addiction.

> Who you have chosen to surround yourself with, the environment you decide to plant yourself in, has the potential to limit you or unlock you.

These relationships may be keeping you from flourishing and livin' the dream that God designed you to live. God's plan is for you to have a bright, purpose-filled, prosperous future. My question is: Are the environments in your life pushing you in that direction? If your relationships aren't making you better, if they're not inspiring you and causing you to grow, you need to make some changes. You may need to pull some weeds and stop hanging out with people who bring out the worst in you and cause you to compromise. Your purpose is too great to waste with people or in environments that are not adding value to your life. If a friend is consistently pulling you down, causing you to compromise, have the courage to lovingly create some distance and slowly begin to step away from them.

What you're not willing to walk away from is where you'll stop growing, possibly even miss out on the things God wants to bring into your life. We have to make some difficult decisions to cultivate and develop our soil, and that often means removing unhealthy relationships so we can experience the healthier, stronger, better relationships God has prepared for us. These times of separating yourself from the wrong people can be tough. I've had to walk through them. These seasons can be lonely, but you can't see them as a time of losing things or losing people. You have to see these seasons as making room for God's best. You can't give something up for God without Him giving you back more in return. You are putting yourself in a position to reach your full potential. You are developing your soil and taking care of what God has put in you.

> What you're not willing to walk away from is where you'll stop growing.

Matthew 9 provides an excellent example of this. Jesus went to pray for a little girl who had died. When he arrived at the house, everyone in the crowd that had gathered was crying and upset. Jesus stepped in and told them the child wasn't dead, that she was just sleeping. They began to laugh and mock Jesus, so He told them to leave the house. He only allowed the parents and Peter, James, and John to stay. He then looked at the little girl and spoke to her, and she miraculously came back to life. Now, why did Jesus have the others leave? He was God. He'd already performed miracles in the midst of thousands. It was because He was showing us the importance of having the right environment and an inner circle or team that supports your faith. At times, you have to make changes in your team to make room for a miracle, for God's best. Some people will talk you out of your dreams if you allow it.

Their doubt, negativity, and sarcasm can rub off on you. You have to set some boundaries. You have to understand that God wants to do some miracles in and through your life, and the team and environment you choose to surround yourself with can make all the difference.

Change Your Environment

In one of my first workplaces, I would often go out to lunch with a group of other staff members. We would explore new places together, talk about sports, and have a good time. But one day this group began talking about our manager, and how they didn't like the way he was leading. This became the topic of our discussion *every* time we went out. Even though some of what they were saying was true, I wasn't comfortable with the gossip and talking behind our manager's back. So I mustered up the courage and told them that I wasn't comfortable being a part of these conversations. I felt that if we weren't a part of the solution, then what we were doing wasn't okay. I had to fight through the mind games that said I was being "holier than thou," that I'd be shunned, that it would somehow backfire on me, but I had to lovingly distance myself from that group the best I knew how. I didn't tell anyone. I just changed my environment. That was difficult because it often meant going to lunch alone for a season. Six months later, for reasons unrelated to me, those same employees were let go and I was promoted. It was a dramatic change, but as I look back, I can see why everything unfolded the way it did.

What you carry is too valuable to allow others to shrink it down with gossip, negativity, and cynicism. I would have missed out on an important opportunity if I had not changed my environment. I wonder what could be waiting for you if you changed your environment. Plant yourself in the right soil. Get around people who will lift you and lift others. Get around people who will make you better, who will call you higher, who will challenge you.

In the Old Testament, Moses sent twelve spies to scout out the Promised Land and report back on the condition of the land that God had promised the Israelites. Of the twelve spies, ten came back with a negative report, saying that there was no chance they could take the land, that the people there were too strong. They said their attempt would most definitely end in defeat. Even though God

> What you carry is too valuable to allow others to shrink it down with gossip, negativity, and cynicism.

had promised them the victory, and even though the other two spies, Joshua and Caleb, declared that they were well able to take the land, those ten negative reports spread throughout the camp. It didn't take long before all two million people were discouraged, complaining, and demanding that Moses take them back to Egypt. An entire generation of Israelites got stuck in fear and unbelief, and they never made it into the Promised Land.

What happened here? That negative environment kept their seed from flourishing. The soil was toxic with unbelief. For you to live the dream, you can't hang around "can't do it" people, "not going to happen" people, "that dream is too big" people. You can't hang around with people who say, "I don't see how you can get well. I don't see how you can break that addiction. I don't see how you can have a healthy marriage." Do yourself a favor and find some Joshuas and Calebs for your dream team. Find people who will fan your flame, instead of throwing water on it. Find people who will stand with you in faith, people who will call the

greatness out of you, who won't let you get stuck or settle. It may
be just a few people, but I promise that you will grow in purpose
and potential.

I described in chapters 2 and 4 how
my life changed during the summer of
1998 when I surrendered my life to
God. Up until then, I had spent most
of the weekends during my teen years
doing things I'm not proud of. That's
all I knew. I honestly was a product

> Find people who
> will fan your flame,
> instead of throwing
> water on it.

of the environment of friends with whom I was hanging out. I
was simply doing what I saw all of them doing. If you wanted to
have fun on Friday nights, you partied, and from what I knew,
that was the only option. A major reason my world changed was
because the soil of my heart changed, but so did the soil around
me. As a new believer, I realized that if I wanted to reach my full
potential, I had to begin to pursue different environments. For
a season it often meant spending Friday nights alone, which was
really hard for me.

But I discovered that even though the numbers in my circle
got smaller, the quality got better. Dan Hade, who invited me to
the summer camp where I first believed, became a close friend
and encourager. I met Chad Bruegman, Shawn Johnson, and Matt
Zachary, who were stronger in their faith than me and had been
following Jesus longer than me. Over time, we grew close. We
started hanging out consistently, attending church services and
small groups together. They taught me how to pray and showed
me that I could have fun without getting drunk. They walked with
me through tough seasons, called me higher, and wouldn't let me
settle or compromise. Those guys became the good soil that my
future needed. To this day, these guys are some of my best friends

and are one of the main reasons I am who I am. Had my circle not changed, had I not pursued a healthier environment, I know what God wanted to do in and through me would have been limited.

Lifters

It's one thing to fight for your future, and it's another thing to know you have people in the corner of your life who are fighting for you. It's important that we understand that our destiny requires every ounce of what we possess. But there will be seasons of your life that will also require someone else fighting for you and lifting you.

> There will be seasons of your life that will also require someone else fighting for you and lifting you.

In Acts 3, a man who had been crippled from birth was lying by the temple gate begging for money. The apostle Peter came by and said, "I don't have any money for you, but in the name of Jesus, rise up and walk." But nothing happened. The man just looked at Peter, thinking, *What do you mean, rise and walk? I'm crippled. I can't walk.* That could have been the end of the story. Peter could have thought, *I did my part, but that didn't work, so it's on to the next assignment.* But he didn't rush to the next thing on his schedule. Peter took the man by the right hand and lifted him up, and as he did, the man's feet and ankle bones were healed.

I love this! I love that Peter didn't let the man stay down. He prayed for him, but then he also pulled him up.

You need some people around you who are like Peter, a dream team that won't let you stay down. We all need people in our lives who love us so much, they won't let us settle and make excuses. They won't let you stay discouraged, or stay addicted, or let you give up on your dream. You need people in your life who will say graciously, "Get up!" and lift you. You had a disappointment? Get up in God's grace! God has a new beginning for you. You've lost something? Get up! God is about to restore it. You're discouraged because you're still single? Get up! Remain content in your faith. God is preparing the right person. You're struggling with your finances? Get up! God is about to open the windows of Heaven. You need people who will help pull you into your destiny. Or better yet, you need some friends who will tear a roof off for you.

Tearing Roofs Off

In Mark 2, when people heard that Jesus had come home to Capernaum, they gathered in such large numbers that there was no room left in the house to hear Him preach the word. At that time, it says, "Some men came, bringing to him a paralyzed man, carried by four of them" (v. 3 NIV). While we don't know the cause of this man's paralysis in the lower half of his body, it is usually caused by an extreme injury or disease of the spinal cord. It's safe to say that this man was stuck to his mat. Hearing where Jesus was, these four friends carried him to the house, but when they arrived, the house was so packed, they couldn't get in. I can imagine the paralyzed man saying, "Hey, guys, it's fine. You tried. Just take me home." But they didn't settle. They didn't stop. They walked around the house, looking for another entrance, but there were no other openings. They could faintly hear Jesus teaching inside, and it motivated them again. Then suddenly, one of the four looked up to the roof and devised a plan. It is unclear exactly how they got the man up and onto the roof, but they did. What then? I imagine they looked at one another, and one man said, "Yup, we're going to have to tear this roof off!" You need some people in your life who aren't afraid to tear a roof off for you, who aren't afraid to get their hands dirty to help you. You need people around you who won't judge you for where you are, but who love you too much not to let you stay where you are. You need a few people who will fight for you. These four friends refused to allow walls and discomfort to keep them from getting their friend to an opportunity.

When was the last time the paraplegic had seen his neighborhood and city from the elevation of that roof? He hadn't even gotten into the house yet, but because of his friends, his perspective was elevated. I can imagine as the four men were digging into the roof to create a hole for him to go through, he was taking in the view. He saw his world, his neighborhood, even his own house from a new perspective. You need relationships in your life that will elevate your vision beyond your current circumstances, that elevate your thinking. We often need others to help us see things that we can't see by ourself. We need to get around people and allow the way they live and treat us to cause us to see ourself and our surroundings differently.

> You need a few people who will fight for you.

As the four friends began to dig, pieces of tile, clay, and wood fell on people gathering in the room below, interrupting whatever was happening at the moment. Then they lowered their paraplegic friend down through this makeshift hole. I imagine that all four of these men wanted to hear and encounter Jesus and had needs they wanted Jesus to meet, but they just lowered the crippled man down. They stayed on the roof and were simply happy and content with their friend getting the miracle he needed. You need friends who will fight for you to get in, and who will stand back and love it! The Bible says that Jesus saw *their faith* and told the man, "Your sins are forgiven. Pick up your mat and go." The man stood up, grabbed his mat, and met up with his four buddies outside the house and had one incredible walk home! Let me ask you, do you have people in your life who will stand in the gap for you? People who will carry you when you can't seem to go on any farther? Who are the people of faith whom you can count on when your faith is running low?

> Who are the people of faith whom you can count on when your faith is running low?

I once received an unexpected phone call from my dad, who'd always been in great health, very active, and always positive. But this call felt different from the start. He told me that he'd gone for a doctor's checkup, and they discovered an issue with his heart. To my dad's surprise, he had suffered a heart attack twelve months earlier and didn't even realize it. Now, they needed to address the damage and work quickly to treat it. This was the most serious health issue my father had ever faced, and as he was telling me, I couldn't help but get emotional. As tears welled up in my eyes, I prayed for him and encouraged him. When I hung up the phone, I was stunned. I immediately told my wife about what was going on with my dad, and then I decided to text my friends Chad and Sonny and ask them to pray for him. They had known my dad, aka "the Rock," for twenty years, and had grown very fond of him. These were the texts I received back:

> We love the Rock and we're gonna be praying for him every morning till he's fine!

We got you, Bro. God's got you too. But we're
doing the *heavy lifting* on this one.

I read that last line and lost it. It felt as though a hundred
pounds had been lifted off my shoulders. It wasn't just the power
of their prayers. It was the fact that they were telling me to count
on their faith. They knew I was tired, that my faith was running
low, and I needed to borrow some of their faith for my dad. We all
need people who are willing to tear some roofs off for us. People
who, when necessary, will do the heavy lifting for us.

Elevators

If you want to live the dream, you have to have some elevators in
your life. Elevators take people to places they couldn't go on their
own. As with those four friends, you need people who fight for
you and create opportunities for you. They make you better.

I've had the honor and privilege of working with those who
have elevated me, and for over fifteen years at Lakewood Church,
I've been able to learn and glean from Pastor Joel Osteen from
afar. However, within the last five years or so, our relationship
has deepened. A few years ago, we started working out together.
Some days we lift weights in the gym, and other days we play tennis. (By the way, he's a beast in the weight room and a freakishly
good athlete.) What I discovered is that he is the same man off the
platform as he is on it. It doesn't matter if he is spotting me on my
last rep or returning one of my tennis serves; he is always encouraging me. I could hit the tennis ball completely over the park's
fence, and he would have something positive to say about my
swing or technique. He typically beats me two out of every three
games, but I always leave feeling great! That's just who he is. And

his belief in me goes beyond the gym and the tennis court. There are few times after I've spoken in a service or meeting when he doesn't send me an articulate text message telling me not just that it was good, but taking the time to tell me *why* it was good. To me, Joel is an elevator. He elevates my thinking by how he lives and carries himself.

A while ago, Joel was going to be the main speaker at a significant event, and he asked me to go with him on the trip. We flew into the city, and the organization had a driver pick us up at the airport. We got into the backseat of the car and proceeded to drive to the event. I could tell Joel had a lot on his mind. I anticipated a very quiet drive so he could focus on his message. But after a few minutes of silence, Joel asked the driver where he was from and how long he had lived in that city. Their conversation lasted the entire length of the drive to the event. By the time we got there, we knew everything there was to know about our driver. Now, Joel isn't an extrovert by nature. I knew he was making a concerted effort to connect with this man. He could have chosen to relax and ride in silence to the event, which would have been understandable, but he didn't. He did the opposite. Even on our way back from the event, he laughed with and encouraged the driver. What thousands of people saw that day was Joel getting on a stage, under the lights, and doing something great in front of a huge crowd. What I saw was him being great both on

> Get around people who are great. People of character who walk in integrity. People who walk in humility. Friends who encourage you and elevate your thinking.

and off the stage. Here was a man caring not only about the thousands, but about the one as well. That's being a man of humility, generosity, and compassion. I could tell many similar stories, particularly of him fighting for me and my family. Times off the stage that inspired me and that elevated my thinking. These are the reasons I'm honored to call him my mentor, pastor, and friend.

Why tell you this? Don't just pursue and get around people who do great things. Get around people who are great. People of character who walk in integrity. People who walk in humility. Friends who encourage you and elevate your thinking.

Saving You from You

My wife is at the center of my dream team. She looks out for me and protects me. I know that I have blind spots. There are areas in my life that I may not see. There are habits or perspectives that are unhealthy. There are attitudes and tendencies I may not always realize I have. Summer knows my heart, and she knows I want to be a man of integrity and continue to grow. So even when it's hard for her, she chooses to protect me.

One night I was watching ESPN, and she was going to bed early. She called out from the bedroom and asked if I could come in for a second. She said, "Hey, the other day when we were talking with that couple over dinner"—I immediately knew what she was talking about—"I don't think the way you talked to them about that other person was right and honoring. Be careful. I love you. Good night."

I just stood at the door wrestling with what she'd said.

As hard as it was to hear it, I knew she was right. Summer doesn't save me from other people necessarily. She often saves me from me. I'm grateful that she loves me enough to speak the truth to me. She's not pushing my dreams down or limiting my potential.

No, just the opposite. She's actually protecting my dreams and my destiny. She's elevating me. She's pulling me higher.

Life jackets are given to rescue people. I've given Summer a life jacket. Sometimes you need to give a life jacket, so to speak, to someone whom you love and trust. Give it to someone who knows you and has your best interests in mind. It's good to look at someone (as I have with Summer) and say, "If you see any blind spots in my life, please tell me. If you see me acting out of character or doing something that's unhealthy or detrimental to

> Whom do you need to give a life jacket to today?

my destiny, please tell me. Keep me accountable. I want to live the best version of myself." I have other people in my life to whom I have given a life jacket and asked to rescue me from me. I know I can't reach my full potential unless I allow others who love me to speak into my life.

Whom do you need to give a life jacket to today? Whom can you give permission to protect you from you? This isn't someone who is squashing your dream. No, change your perspective. These are people who are designed to preserve it.

Friends in Unusual Places

You might be in a season of your life when you don't even know where to look for your dream team. I believe that if you ask God to connect you to your dream team, He will. In fact, you may discover them in some unusual places.

One summer day in 2009, I stopped at a gas station near our house to fill my tank. As I stood by the pump, I noticed a man who looked about my age parked with his boat, preparing with his daughter for what appeared to be a day on the lake. As he walked out of the gas station with ice, I don't know what came over me, but I felt compelled to walk over and introduce myself. I didn't really have a plan, so I simply asked, "How's the lake?" It seemed like a good icebreaker and broad enough to kick-start a brief conversation. He told me his name was Mike and that he had just started to take his boat out with his family and loved it. He and his wife, Amy, were about the same age as Sum and me, and they had a two-year-old daughter named Hannah. We talked for about ten minutes, connected immediately, and exchanged phone numbers.

A few days later, he texted me and invited us out on their boat on the weekend. I told him we would love to, but a few days later, we began to have second thoughts. We didn't even know these people, and we were going to spend hours with them on a boat?! If it were to get weird or awkward, we had no escape. Come to find out, Mike and Amy were having the same second thoughts, but we all decided to push through and roll the dice. We had an incredible time that day, and two hours ended up being five hours together. We found ourselves spending a few Saturdays in a row on the boat with them. Our relationship grew. Days on the boat together evolved into PS4 *Rock Band* sessions (a PlayStation video game for you non-gamers), which evolved into taking vacations and trips with them. Years later, we were spending Thanksgivings and Fourth of Julys together.

> No matter where God takes you, He will supply divine relationships.

It's been over thirteen years since we met at the gas station, and a lot has changed. All of our jobs have evolved, we've added more kids to our crew, but the one thing that hasn't changed is the steady source of love, strength, and encouragement we have shared together. We have become like family. What am I saying? No matter where God takes you, He will supply divine relationships. We left our family in 2007 to follow our purpose and chase our destiny, but God brought the right people into our lives. I believe He will do the same for you. He knows whom you need for every season, and He will connect you with the right people. So the next time you are pumping gas at a station, look around. You may just meet your next dream team member.

Unforeseen Blessings

We are all a by-product of mentors, coaches, teachers, and loved ones who have invested in us over the years. There have been people who took the time to breathe life into us, spent their time and energy to make sure we were growing, and sacrificed when we didn't know it to make sure we had the best opportunities and chances to succeed. We need to celebrate them and let them know how important they have been.

From my childhood up to now, there have been many people whom God has put in my life to inspire, encourage, and bring out the best in me. There was Mrs. Douglas, my second grade teacher. Then there was Coach Don Tobias, my baseball coach when I was twelve years old. There was Mr. Goodwine the coolest, "swaggiest" gym teacher, who wore new Jordans with matching Nike gym suits every day.

But George "JA" Weatherall was my first real mentor. He lived down the street from us and was the neighborhood ringleader of sports when I was growing up. He was a few years older than the rest of us kids, and he had this gift of pulling us all together to play pickup games. I have fond memories of home run derbies, tackle football, and "21" basketball in the neighborhood. JA was the key. He not only arranged these games, but taught us things such as not to quit, how to let go of mistakes, and to forgive a brother (that was required a lot). He did this all through the sandlot games we played that sparked a love for sports in all of us. When many kids in my school and neighborhood were getting into drugs and falling into negative habits, I was too busy playing sports with JA and the crew. Our neighborhood wasn't the greatest. We had drug houses on our street. Gang violence was close. Yet JA kept many of us out of trouble, and he was the first one besides my father who told me I could be great.

Today, I'm surrounded by people who are smarter than me, wiser than me, and have achieved more than me. Dr. Paul Osteen, for example, has been a mentor for years and helped officiate our wedding. Besides personifying Christlike character and compassion, he has shown me what it means to lead and live with strength and humility. I'll never forget the advice he gave me about being a great leader and father. He said, "Nick, be quick to say you're sorry to your kids, your wife, and those you do life with." I've watched Dr. Paul exemplify this. I just wish I could get more of it. He spends almost half of the year in Africa doing medical missionary work. The man is a legend, and I wouldn't be half of who I am if it were not for his encouragement, example, and wisdom in my life.

And then there's Tauren Wells, an internationally known Christian singer and songwriter. One Halloween, Summer and I were taking our kids around our neighborhood to get loads of candy. Every year, as hard as we try, we can't keep up. Their drive for more sugar always puts them a few houses in front of us. On this night, Denver came running back to us and said he was at a house and the man he met asked if he was Denver. He said yes, and the man told him to tell me that he said hello. I asked Denver to take me to the man's house so I could see who it was. The man turned out to be Tauren. I had known Tauren for years, but never knew he and his wife, Lorna, lived just a few blocks from our house. We laughed about the incident and talked for a while, and they invited us over for dinner soon after that Halloween night. That sparked a close friendship that we have built. Tauren and Lorna have been an unforeseen blessing in our lives. Their encouragement, love, and friendship mean the world to us. They have prayed with us, protected us, and been there for us when we needed loyal friends.

Sometimes you have to walk away from certain relationships. Sometimes you have to seek out your dream team. Other times, when you chase your purpose, God brings them to you. They surprise you! As with the Wells family, they just might be closer than you think!

Be Intentional about Your Team

Every dream needs a team. Every seed needs a good environment to grow. Take some time today to think about who is in your life and what your "soil" looks like. I'm asking you to focus on soil development. Some of your seed can't grow in the soil you are currently in, and it's time to make the first move. It's time to change your aquarium. If you're the smartest, most talented, sharpest one in your circle, it may be time to pursue another circle. You have more to become; you have greatness inside that a new environment can facilitate and bring out. Be intentional about your dream team.

> Take some time today to think about who is in your life and what your "soil" looks like.

The good news is that your past doesn't have to stop you. As I did, you may have made some bad relationship decisions and put yourself in bad environments and circles in the past. You were surrounded by people who influenced you to compromise or told you who you couldn't become and why you weren't going to be successful. But your seed is still alive, and you're reading this for a reason. Pursue the right environments and relationships, and I believe you will see your dream team take shape and take another step toward reaching your full potential!

CHAPTER SEVEN

THE POWER OF CONSISTENCY

Find Your Miracle in the Mundane

recently read something fascinating about how the Chinese bamboo tree grows. Like any plant, the bamboo tree requires fertile soil and sunshine. But even more important is its need for consistent watering and care. Here's why. In its first year, you will see no visible signs of activity. In the second year, again, no growth above the soil. The third and fourth years? Still nothing. During this period, it's easy to wonder if the efforts and consistent care are working. Is anything happening? And then in the fifth year. Breakthrough. Explosive growth. The Chinese bamboo tree breaks ground and grows ninety feet in just six weeks! The question is: Does it take six weeks or five years and six weeks to grow ninety feet? It's easy to think that it happened almost overnight, but the truth is that because of consistent care and attention over a span of five years, the root system grew and developed to sustain the height of the tree when it sprouted.

When it comes to our lives, it's easy to assume that growth, new levels, and promotion all come quickly and as a result of a moment of work or faith. Yes, at times things can change suddenly, but that's usually a by-product of consistent seasons of faith and action. What am I saying? The same consistency required for the bamboo tree to reach its full potential is the same consistency we need to possess in order to reach our full potential.

God is into consistency.

Look at creation. The sunrise and the sunset. Consistent. Look at the seasons. Spring, summer, fall, and winter. Consistent. The tides of the ocean. In and out. Consistent.

Look at how He made us. Listen to your heartbeat. Consistency. How you breathe in and out. Consistency.

We were made in the image of God, which means we were made to be consistent. We were made to have and be consistent leaders, friends, parents, and workers. The psalmist says, "Make my steps steady through your promise" (Psalm 119:133 CSB). The apostle Paul says, "Therefore, my beloved, be steadfast, immovable, always excelling in the work of the Lord, because you know that in the Lord your labor is not in vain" (1 Corinthians 15:58 NRSV). In other words, consistency is what takes us from one level to the next. It is required if we want to reach our God-given potential. I didn't say perfection is required. Consistency is required.

Shine in the Shadows

Often, what keeps us from continuing to do the things we know we should be doing—whether it's showing up to work on time, doing the inventory check, or vacuuming the floor—is that we think many of the "hidden" things in life are insignificant. No one really sees or notices these things, so why do them consis-

> Why give our all every day? There are miracles in the mundane places of your life.

tently? Why give our all every day? Let me encourage you today: There are miracles in the mundane places of your life. Change your perspective of the seemingly "small" things you do at work or the "small" things you do for your kids and family. I encourage you to shine in the shadows! Shine when no one claps. Shine when there's no spotlight. Being consistent when you want to give up, when no one seems to appreciate you, is passing the test and showing God you can handle the blessings and opportunities He has planned for you in your future.

> God sees every little thing you do in secret, and He will reward you!

Are you in a season where you find yourself doing a lot of tasks in the background? Let me encourage you that what you do right now in the shadows matters. It may be unseen, but that doesn't mean it isn't significant. Don't underestimate the menial, behind-the-scenes things you are doing.

Shine in the shadows. Be your best even if no one celebrates you. God sees every little thing you do in secret, and He will reward you!

Keep On Keepin' On

In Galatians 6:9, the apostle Paul says the qualifications of reaping a harvest of blessing aren't talent, good looks, or knowing the right people. It is simply not giving up on doing good. You don't need talent to be consistent. Anyone can be consistent. We all have the opportunity.

Noah was given the immense job of building the ark in the book of Genesis. God gave him a list of specific instructions to carry out. "So make yourself an ark of cypress wood; make rooms in it and coat it with pitch inside and out. This is how you are to build it: The ark is to be three hundred cubits long, fifty cubits wide and thirty cubits high. Make a roof for it, leaving below the roof an opening one cubit high all around. Put a door in the side of the ark and make lower, middle and upper decks" (Genesis 6:14–16 NIV). This was a huge boat with a roof, multiple decks, and a lot of rooms.

Scholars don't agree on how long it took Noah to build the ark, but we know it took many decades. He didn't have power drills or electric saws, Bobcats or heavy-duty logging equipment. He was working with some simple tools. I imagine that after a week of hard work, the enormity of the project set in. I also imagine that after a few weeks, his friends and neighbors began criticizing him and making jokes. If this were me, after week four, I would want to quit. It wasn't only the hard work, but no one had ever even seen the style of boat that he was attempting to build. It didn't make sense, it was overwhelmingly difficult, and there was no hint of rain. Noah, however, kept on keepin' on. He just kept pushing forward on the building. One deck and room at a time, year after year after year, until one day, when he was putting the finishing touches on the door, it started to rain. His work wasn't in vain. His family and pairs of all the earth's animal life came aboard. I'm sure Noah breathed a huge sigh of relief when the story says the "LORD shut him in" (Genesis 7:16 NIV). He completed the job; the human race and the animal kingdom were saved.

There are areas in all of our lives that feel very monotonous and mundane. Some are boring, to be quite honest. Often our jobs involve doing the same things every day. Filling out the spreadsheets, surveying the land, meeting with clients. There's mowing the lawn, sorting the kids' clothes, grocery shopping, and cleaning the house. It doesn't matter what you do; over time it can become tiring and you

> Keep doing what you can do until God does what you can't do.

can feel as though you are stuck without making any progress or seeing any fruit from all your efforts. Here's a lesson from Noah. Keep doing what you can do until God does what you can't do.

Think about all the animals making their way to the boat. The cheetahs get there first, then the lions, gazelles, and horses stroll in. Birds of all kinds fly in while snakes slither their way inside, and after all the animals finally make their way in, there is still one left. Imagine all the animals were packed in the boat, and they are ready for the rain, but wait! Noah sees something inching its way to the ramp! "Stop! Hold on! Don't lift the gate! I see something. It's the snails." Those snails came from what seemed like a place far, far away. They wanted to quit, but their future family was dependent upon them. Even if they were the last ones aboard, they had to keep on. The snails finally crawl into the safety of the boat, the door shuts, and the rain begins to pour. Those snails refused to give up. They probably showed up last, but they made it!! Every time you see a snail, know that its ancestors from long ago kept on keepin' on!

The power of consistency is crucial because you never know when the breakthrough, promotion, healing, or next level is coming. Consistently having a good attitude, forgiving, encouraging, working hard, and being your best leads you to divine appointments and set times of favor.

> They cast ninety-nine times, wanted to quit, but Jesus showed up and supernaturally touched the hundredth cast.

In chapter 2, we considered the story of Jesus going to restore Peter when he reverted back to fishing in John 21. Let's look at it from a different perspective. The disciples fished all night and caught nothing. Someone shows up on the shore in the early morning and tells them to cast their net on the right side of the boat. Now imagine the disciples. These guys are fishermen by trade and know their craft. They already cast the net in that area of water all night. Like ninety-nine times! I'm sure some of the disciples want to tell whoever is yelling fishing tips to get lost. Jesus says, "One more time, boys. They're on the right side of your boat." I imagine they reluctantly lift the net and drop it down. But suddenly the net begins to tug! Out of nowhere big fish fill the net. It requires all of them to hold the net in place, and it's too heavy to pull into the boat. They are stunned and exhausted by this miraculous catch. What happened? They cast ninety-nine times, wanted to quit, but Jesus showed up and supernaturally touched the hundredth cast.

You could be on your ninety-ninth cast to get that promotion or job opportunity. You could be on your ninety-ninth prayer for your husband. You could be on your ninety-ninth day of being sick. Keep on keepin' on! One more step of faith, one more application, one more prayer of faith could be the difference for you and the breakthrough you are believing for.

It's Worth the Wait

Most likely, you are doing your best to remain consistent in areas of your life because you have your sights set on something

THE POWER OF CONSISTENCY

or someone. So what is it that you are waiting for? Who are you waiting for in this season of your life? Are you single, waiting for a husband or a wife? Have you turned in your job application and now you're waiting for a call for employment? Are you holding on to your degree and waiting for direction? Are you waiting on a promise or a dream, a healing or business partner? The question isn't if you're waiting for something. The better question is, How are you waiting?

I was recently on a flight to Chicago, and as we descended and began our approach to the airport, all of a sudden I felt the plane slow and begin to turn. We went into a very slow circular pattern. This went on for about fifteen minutes, which felt like eternity. I didn't know what was going on, and my anxiety slowly increased with every turn. Then the pilot came on the PA speaker and told us that we had arrived a little early, the runways were not clear for us to land yet, and we'd been in a holding pattern but would land shortly. He said to sit back and relax, because we still would be getting to our gate on time. I was so grateful to hear the update. Oftentimes in life, there are seasons when it seems we're waiting in a holding pattern. We have a dream or we're holding on to a promise. You can almost see it, but you're not there yet. You want to arrive, but you're waiting, and you may not always get to hear God's voice giving you the reason for the wait. Here's the thing. That plane I was on wasn't lost or off track. There was nothing wrong with it. There were just things we didn't see that weren't in alignment yet. It was not our time yet.

> One more step of faith, one more application, one more prayer of faith could be the difference for you and the breakthrough you are believing for.

What we didn't realize in that moment on the plane was all the things the traffic controller had to consider, move around, and guide into place so we could arrive safely at our appropriate time. In our lives we see things not changing. Things aren't happening as quickly as we hoped and it feels as though we're going in circles. What we don't see is all the other things and people that our purpose is attached to and impacted by that must first get into alignment. What am I saying? God is the author and finisher of our faith. He's the controller. He has a plan, and every season that we are in is strategic. My challenge is for you to change your perspective of the season you are in now. There is deep purpose in the waiting. You may not feel anything changing. It may feel as though you are going in circles. But while you are waiting, God is working. He's working in people around you, and He's working in you, making sure His plan for your life unfolds in His timing.

In Mark 5, a man named Jairus, a synagogue leader, was desperate. His twelve-year-old daughter was dying. He came to Jesus and pleaded with Him to come and heal her. Jesus agreed and began walking with him to his house. But as they were walking through a huge crowd, a woman with a twelve-year-old bleeding issue pushed through the crowd and possibly Jairus. She silently touched Jesus' robe, and by faith she pulled healing power from Him and was healed. It was a miracle. Jesus stopped and silenced the crowd to have a conversation with her.

But wait. While all this was happening, where was Jairus? What happened to his need?

It seems as though he'd been pushed into the background of someone else's miraculous moment. Jairus was watching as his hopes were disrupted, and every second was counting for his daughter. As he was waiting, he had a choice—to stay or leave. It would have been easy to leave. He had good reasons to give up.

He could have thought that others in the crowd would call out for healing. He could have thought that Jesus had forgotten about what He promised He would do. Did he get passed over? Perhaps this woman took the only twelve-year-old miracle off the shelf of Jesus' inventory? Then on top of Jairus's own mind games while he was waiting, friends came and told him that his daughter had died and he shouldn't bother Jesus anymore. Despite all of this, Jairus waited. He stayed. He kept his eyes on Jesus and trusted Him.

After Jesus had healed the woman, He said to Jairus, "Don't be afraid. I know you think it's over. I know others are trying to talk you out of it. I know you're sick of waiting, but stay in faith. I haven't forgotten about you. Take Me to your house. Just believe." They walked directly to his house, and when they arrived, Jesus took Jairus and his wife and a few of His disciples and went into the room where the girl was lying lifeless. Holding her hand, He told the little girl to get up. The girl immediately stood up and walked around. Everyone was overwhelmed and totally amazed by the miracle.

> Jairus asked for a healing, but what he experienced was a resurrection! While he was waiting, the miracle was growing.

What if we asked Jairus about that delay on the way? What would he say? I'm sure that without hesitation he would tell us that the interruption was purposeful. He was glad he didn't listen to people who told him that he was crazy and should have just given up. He would say it was definitely worth the wait.

What's powerful is that Jairus asked for a healing, but what he experienced was a resurrection! The miracle was much greater than he thought. While he was waiting, the miracle was growing. While you're waiting on your promise, God is working, moving, and preparing the promise. And guess what? It's going to be bigger and better than what you could even imagine.

You know what else grew that quite possibly is the greatest blessing in this story? Jairus's faith. His ability to trust Jesus and walk with Jesus into the unknown, not on his timetable but on Jesus' timetable. When he thought nothing was changing around him, God was changing things in him— deepening his faith, character, and trust. God was changing who he was. Changing how he would wait for things in the future, and changing how he would see other delays that would come into his life. What God does in us while we wait is just as important as the thing we're waiting for. So trust God. If you are waiting for something, the change that's happening in you is worth it.

> What God does in us while we wait is just as important as the thing we're waiting for.

You Are Being Prepared

If we are honest, I think most of us would say that waiting times feel as though we're being kept from something, being held back from something. In reality, God is preparing us for something.

Scholars say that Moses was around eighty years old when God spoke to him through a burning bush in Exodus 3. It was a call to arise and step into his destiny. God approached him and made it very clear that He had chosen him to lead the Israelites out of Egyptian captivity. God then did a series of miracles that He displayed through Moses and delivered His people out of Pharaoh's control. However, after Moses had led the people through the Red Sea, he found himself faced with a difficult leadership predicament. He would have to lead two million people through a very rough and desolate wilderness. How was he going to chart this? He didn't have Google Maps or satellite imaging. It seemed that he wasn't equipped for this chapter of leadership. But the wilderness he was about to lead the Israelites through was the same land where he had spent most of his adult life as a shepherd. This wasn't foreign territory for Moses. He knew it very well. In those waiting years, God had Moses gaining firsthand knowledge of the land, so he could lead his people through it later. It may have looked as though he was waiting for or being held back from something, but in actuality he was being prepared and equipped for something.

Keep a good attitude even when it's not happening on your timetable. It may feel as though people are holding you back, or you are being overlooked, but you are not. As with Moses, God is equipping you to handle and sustain where He is going to take you.

After Samuel had anointed David to be the next king of Israel, David had to wait thirteen years to actually see it come to reality. God could have taken him straight to the throne, but He didn't. David went back to taking care of his father's sheep. It seemed insignificant. It wasn't something someone with a king's calling should be doing. But those years of shepherding sheep were preparing him to one day shepherd God's people. David passed the test. He had to show God he could take care of his father's sheep before God could trust him to take care of His sheep, the Israelites.

There were many things that David learned while waiting. While being a shepherd, he learned how to physically defend the sheep he was entrusted with, to fight off lion attacks and even kill a bear. All of these moments prepared him for his future. One day, this shepherd with a king's calling took his three soldier brothers a provision of food, doing a menial task, when he came face-to-face with a giant named Goliath. This giant who had all of Israel's bravest soldiers intimidated didn't cause David to flinch. David picked up his sling and a few stones and took down the giant. This event was the catalyst that thrust David into his destiny to be the king of Israel. What happened? All of those years fighting predators and protecting the sheep entrusted into his care had prepared him for this moment. Goliath didn't intimidate David because he had already fought lions, bears, and other threats.

What if David had overlooked those years in the fields, regarding them as unimportant and insignificant? What if he'd had a bad attitude and slacked off because he didn't care about the welfare of the sheep? Clearly, he wouldn't have been prepared for Goliath, and he would have missed his opportunity. Each of us has something we want to accomplish, something we want to experience—a dream, a marriage, owning our own business. We have to resist the temptation to overlook the place and position God has us in now. There are things right now that He's doing in you that will equip you to sustain and handle what He has coming your way. Pass the test. Have a good attitude. Be excellent where you are. Fight against jealousy, and celebrate others' success in the meantime. God is preparing you for something bigger than you can imagine. It's very powerful when you can say, "God, I not only trust Your ways, but I trust Your timing." The mistake we often make as we wait is to get impatient and try to make things happen in our own timing instead of traveling steadily and patiently. We push to get things and take matters into our own hands. We may get what we think is rightfully ours, but it's at the wrong time and it always comes with a cost.

> What if David had overlooked those years in the fields, regarding them as unimportant and insignificant?

Wait with Purpose

I had a good friend in high school named Steve who was a car fanatic. When we were nearly sixteen, we took driver's ed together, and every day he talked about how he couldn't wait to drive. His parents had already bought him a red 5.0 Ford Mustang with a high-performance engine and a nice sound system. It was tricked out, fully loaded. The only rule they had was that he couldn't drive it until he turned sixteen and had passed driver's ed. One Saturday before Steve passed the course, he called me over to his house and wanted to show me something. As I walked into his garage, he pulled back the cover and revealed the beautiful Mustang. He asked if I wanted to take it for a spin. I really wanted to, but I remembered his parents' rule. I told him I would pass, but Steve was so excited that he jumped in the car and pulled it out of the driveway. As soon as he got in the street, he punched the gas. I stood by watching as smoke from the tires surrounded the rear end, and the car immediately started to slide out of control. The rear tires hit the curb so hard and so fast that it flipped the car into the ditch and over on its side. I ran over and immediately checked on Steve. By the looks of the car, I assumed the worst. Miraculously, he walked away from the accident with only a few cuts and bruises, but he did not walk away from his parents. Let's just say he didn't start driving when he turned sixteen.

> Waiting is God's way of preparing.

Sometimes in life we can take what is rightfully ours at the wrong time, as in too early. When we're not prepared to handle it, the thing God has arranged and set aside to bless us can instantly become a burden, and all because we didn't wait for His timing.

Steve wanted his prepared blessing. The problem was, he was unprepared to handle it. Waiting is God's way of preparing.

There are many ways in which we take matters into our own hands, especially when we feel we are falling behind. Our friend is getting married, and we're still single. Our coworkers are getting promoted, and we've been with the business longer. Our kid brother just bought a new house, and we're still in an apartment. Here's the key. What has your name on it will not go to someone else. No matter how hard someone tries to get what's yours, God won't allow it. It doesn't matter how hard people try to manipulate or play politics, you don't have to worry. If it's supposed to be yours, it will come to you. You are not being bypassed. You are not being overlooked. You are not forgotten. What has your name on it will come to you. Don't get discouraged. Grow in patience. Celebrate others. Do your best where you are.

When you meet the person He's prepared for you, you will say, "It was worth the wait." When you see the contract that's being prepared for you now, it will be worth the wait. When you see the new door that opens, you will say it was worth the wait. Not only will it be better than you imagined, but you will also possess the character to handle it.

Back to my flight to Chicago. Up until the point we started waiting, everyone in my row was pretty quiet. No one was talking. Headphones were on, laptops were open, and phones were being scrolled. Everyone was focused on themselves and just getting to our destination. What's interesting is that when we went into our holding pattern, everyone began to talk with one another. We began to ask each other what was going on. Our attention moved from ourselves to our surroundings and one another. The guy sitting next to me began to talk to me about his job and the challenges he was facing, not only with his career path but also with his family. Toward the end of our conversation, he asked me to pray for his career, his family, his marriage, and his kids. It was a special God moment. When we landed, we went our separate ways and didn't reconnect, but maybe that waiting period was designed for that conversation. Perhaps that one prayer made a difference in the trajectory of his family and his destiny. I wonder how many powerful opportunities you might be overlooking while waiting for your promise. It's good to have faith for a future promise, but it's better to wait in the meantime with purpose. Recognize that while God is working in you, He also has filled each day in this season with purpose.

You're Not Waiting Alone

Another thing to consider is that a waiting period may be designed to realign your goals and objectives in life. Maybe the waiting is bringing you back to wanting God more than you want what He can give you. I've experienced this throughout my faith journey—times when waiting allowed me to see the need for His presence more than what He could provide me, even more than His

> Don't reduce God to your next miracle. He's not a superhero. He's more than a miracle worker who shows up and acts on our behalf.

promise. Whenever I'm waiting on something, I'm reminded that more than what I'm waiting for, Jesus is the reward. He's much better than anything I could be waiting for. Jesus can do miracles, provide for all your needs, open doors that no one can shut, but don't reduce Him to that. Don't reduce God to your next miracle. He's not a superhero. He's more than a miracle worker who shows up and acts on our behalf.

> God is your Father, and He wants to be a part of every fiber and fabric of your life.

God is your Father, and He wants to be a part of every fiber and fabric of your life. He can move mountains, but He also wants to move with you. He can silence the enemy of your life, but He also wants to speak to you. He can part the seas, but He also wants to walk with you through them. Sometimes He's quiet, sometimes He's loud, but always for a purpose and always for our good. What am I saying? You don't have to wait alone. He's with you, close and personal. God is directing your steps. He's in control of your life. He has you in the palms of His hands. He's not just the God of the beginning and the end, He's also the God of the middle, and He doesn't waste any time in the waiting. God says, "I am with you and I will protect you wherever you go....I will not leave you until I have finished giving you everything I have promised you" (Genesis 28:15 NLT).

Knowing God is with us in the waiting changes our perspective on the waiting season. This promise should fuel your passion to keep on keepin' on and being consistent right where you are. Choose to shine in the shadows today, to be consistent, especially in the mundane spaces of your life. Consistency is a powerful force that forges strong marriages, builds healthy companies, empowers ministries, and is a key for you to reach your full potential. You may have tried ninety-nine times, but remember what can happen on the hundredth. I'm believing that as you remain faithful and don't give up in doing good, taking the high road, honoring God right where you are, the sun is going to come, the nets will fill in your life, the right opportunities will come your way. I declare as you keep on doing what you can do, the God who is always with you will step in and do what you can't.

Trust His timing, and live the dream while you wait.

CHAPTER EIGHT

FAVOR FOLLOWS YOU

Heaven Has Your Back

When I was in middle school, my older brother, Adam, and I would walk a few miles every day to school and back. He would usually walk with his friends on a certain route, and I would walk with my friends on another route. At the beginning of seventh grade, on my walk home I noticed a group of three older kids who would bully other students. One day, I guess they decided it was my turn. As they approached me, I started freaking out, thinking of a plan to escape. I was walking alone that day, so I didn't have my friends to help. How was I going to get away from the bullies? Before I could attempt to escape, they were in front of me. They stopped me on the sidewalk, and I braced for a fight. I sized them up and figured I might be able to take the smallest kid, but not all three of them at the same time. This was going to get ugly.

Just as the ringleader began to open his mouth, something behind me caught their attention. They stopped and froze, then they turned around and took off running in the opposite direction. I stood there in a bit of a daze. What had just happened? Did they catch a glimpse of my biceps? Did they realize I had started weight training in the seventh grade? What was it? Then I turned around and saw my brother, who was a ninth grader, and two of his huge friends running to get my back! They were ready to fight for me and protect me from the bullies. It was a rescue for the ages, and I was so relieved! Throughout our childhood, my big brother would usually mess with me and pick on me. I get it—it's what big brothers do. But that day he showed his true love and loyalty to me. Those bullies never tried messing with me again. They knew someone bigger and stronger had my back, and he was always looking out for me.

You may be facing opposition today. Maybe it's not a group of bullies, but it's something that feels as though it's going to defeat you or put an end to your career, marriage, or reputation. Let me remind you that you have a great defender and vindicator behind you. You are not alone. As you chart difficulties, as you face opposition, you have all the forces of Heaven on your side.

Heaven…has…your…back!

As we go through life, it's easy to get convinced that sickness, negativity, bad breaks, and unhealthy relationships are following us. But I'm here to encourage you that when you choose to follow Jesus, something else begins to follow you, and it's called "favor." It's not because you've suddenly earned it, but because you are a child of God. David says, "Surely goodness and mercy shall follow me all the days of my life" (Psalm 23:6 NKJV). He also declared: "I can never get away from your presence! If I go up to heaven, you are there; if I go down to the grave, you are there. If I ride the wings of the morning, if I dwell by the farthest oceans, even there your hand will guide me, and your strength will support me" (Psalm 139:7–10 NLT).

If David was convinced of one thing, it's that favor followed him. Sometimes we may feel we're favored because of the people we're in relationship with or because we're with a certain company or live in a certain area. No disrespect to those places and people, but the reason you are blessed is because God's favor is following you. You are a son or a daughter of God. Have you moved to a new state? A new job? A new position? Don't worry. Favor didn't stay in the place you left. No, it followed you.

Favor May Not Look Like Favor

In Matthew 14, after Jesus fed the five thousand, He sent the disciples on a boat to cross the lake in the evening. He told them He would meet up with them later on the other side of the lake. After He'd dismissed the crowd, He went up on a mountain and spent time in prayer well into the middle of the night. Meanwhile, a windstorm rushed down upon the lake and the winds battered the disciples' boat. Catch

> They didn't face a storm because they were doing the wrong thing; they faced a storm when they were doing the right thing.

this. They were obeying Jesus' instructions, but it seemed He'd given them the wrong directions or sent them at the wrong time.

They didn't face a storm because they were doing the wrong thing; they faced a storm when they were doing the right thing. They were right in the center of God's will, yet they were struggling and battling a storm. Just because you are facing a storm of difficulty doesn't necessarily mean you are out of God's will.

> Sometimes what you think is going to destroy you is actually coming to save and protect you.

Watch what happened. Jesus saw what was happening and went out to them, walking on the lake. "When the disciples saw him walking on the lake, they were terrified. 'It's a ghost,' they said, and cried out in fear" (Matthew 14:26 NIV). Just when they thought their trip couldn't get worse, they saw a ghost! Jesus showed up, walking on water, coming to save them, and they thought He was a ghost coming to destroy them. What's my point? Sometimes what you think is going to destroy you is actually coming to save and protect you. In the darkness, Jesus looked like a ghost to them. Favor may not always look like favor when it first arrives. Favor didn't stop on the shoreline. Favor followed them into the middle of the storm. Jesus followed them, walking on top of the raging waves that had them in fear. You may not feel favored today because of what you are in the middle of, but as we see with the disciples, there is nothing that can keep favor from getting to you. In fact, the apostle Paul says "that nothing can ever separate us from God's love. Neither death nor life, neither angels nor demons, neither our fears for today nor our worries about tomorrow—not even the powers of hell can separate us from God's love" (Romans 8:38 NLT).

So now that you know that favor will always follow you, why don't you change your perspective on the storm you are facing?

Could it be that the thing that appears to be setting you back is God's favor protecting you? The breakup of a relationship may not feel good, but later, when you realize how controlling and hurtful the person was, you realize that was God's favor. Getting let go from your job may leave you feeling like the bottom dropped out, but after seeing the company go bankrupt after a few months, you realize that was God's favor. The door of opportunity that you were hoping would open but

> Could it be that the thing that appears to be setting you back is God's favor protecting you?

didn't felt like a setback, but after walking through a better door later, you realize that was God's favor. You have to see that God's favor can come in many different forms, but what doesn't change is the promise that it will follow you.

Favor in the Fire

The life of Joseph is an amazing example of how favor can follow someone. As a young adult, he had a dream deep inside that one day he would rule. Shortly after the dream was planted in his heart, his jealous older brothers plotted to destroy him. They threw him in a pit, intending to kill him, but ended up selling him into slavery. This was not the ideal start to his dream and didn't look like God's favor. It was not what he imagined as the route God would take him to a throne. Despite what it looked like, Joseph would change settings, jobs, and locations, but the Bible says favor followed him everywhere he went.

How about when he was sold into the household of Potiphar, a captain of the guard for Pharaoh? "The Lord was with Joseph, so he succeeded in everything he did as he served in the home of his Egyptian master. Potiphar noticed this and realized that the LORD was with Joseph, giving him success in everything he did. This pleased Potiphar, so he soon made Joseph his personal attendant" (Genesis 39:2–4 NLT). Joseph was definitely not where he wanted to be, but he was favored, and others knew it.

When Potiphar's wife falsely accused him of a crime, Joseph ended up in prison for years. "But the LORD was with Joseph in the prison and showed him his faithful love. And the LORD made Joseph a favorite with the prison warden. Before long, the warden put Joseph in charge of all the other prisoners and over everything that happened in the prison. The warden had no more worries,

> God may not always remove you from the fire, but He will follow you into the fire and favor you all the way through it.

because Joseph took care of everything. The LORD was with him and caused everything he did to succeed" (Genesis 39:21–23 NLT). Again, Joseph was not where he wanted to be. He was in prison, but guess what? He was favored.

Joseph would later interpret dreams while in prison, which led to his interpreting Pharaoh's dream. In one day he moved from being in prison to suddenly being in charge over all of Egypt. Notice how God's favor followed him into places he didn't want to be in. You could say that favor followed him into the fire. God may not always remove you from the fire, but He will follow you into the fire and favor you all the way through it. It's when you follow Jesus and bless those who aren't good to you and forgive and let go of offenses. It's when you serve even though it's not popular, and fight to hold on to your joy even though you see nothing changing. That's when you will experience the favor that carries you through and protects you, and you walk out better, promoted, and stronger.

Joseph was forgotten for thirteen years of his life in Potiphar's house and prison, yet he was favored. You can be forgotten by man but still be favored by God. Even though you are struggling, you are favored. Even though you are hurt, you are favored. Even though you are in debt, you are favored. Don't limit God's favor to a destination. He's with you, and His favor

> You can be forgotten by man but still be favored by God.

follows you everywhere you go. It can anchor you and carry you through the most challenging times. Trust Him. Trust His plan. Take the high road, and let Him promote you. What am I saying? Nothing can stop a person who is followed by favor.

Overtake You

Imagine that there are two people, one whose name is Goodness and one whose name is Mercy. According to Psalm 23, because you are a child of God, their assignment is to follow you. Does it say they work on some days and not on others? No. Just when you are at church? No. It says their job is to follow you *all* the days of your life. As you walk, they walk. When you turn, they turn. When you move, they move. When you get on a plane, they get on a plane. When you make a mistake, do they turn and run away? No, they stay, and they follow you. You are being followed by favor, and there's nothing you can do about it.

The Scripture also says, "And all these blessings shall come upon you and overtake you, because you obey the voice of the Lord your God" (Deuteronomy 28:2 NKJV). Maybe you are battling a sickness? Get ready, because healing is about to overtake you. Maybe you have been battling an addiction? Get ready, because freedom is about to overtake you. Maybe you are feeling weak and worn-out? Get ready, because strength is about to overtake you. When you follow God, you can rest in His promise that favor follows you. It's time to start changing what you are believing and declaring for your life. Start praying, "Father, thank You that I'm prospering in a downturn. I'm flourishing in a famine. The economy may be bad, but You are not limited to the economy. You can get me what I need at the right time. Favor is following me."

This principle is especially important when someone is waiting to meet the right person. Oftentimes I see singles desperately searching for the right person, jumping in and out of relationships, chasing and being chased, feeling that they have to make it happen. Instead of putting all your energy and focus on meeting the right person, focus your attention on becoming the right person. In due season favor (the one you are hoping for) will find you. You can't control when you meet the right person, but you can control what you do and who you become in the meantime. You don't have to stress about finding your spouse, because if you're chasing your life purpose, God will bring the right person to you. While you wait, focus on discovering and growing in the security and confidence of who you are, of getting comfortable in your own skin, of becoming who God has called and designed you to be. Do what you're passionate about, and once in a while take a look around at who's near you.

> You can't control when you meet the right person, but you can control what you do and who you become in the meantime.

There will be a divine time when God brings your spouse *to* you. It will be natural, not rushed, not forced. Favor will overtake you.

Sooner Than Expected

I love Amazon, especially Amazon Prime's fast delivery. I can be a procrastinator at times, and I've needed Prime to come through and bail me out. One Friday, it dawned on me that I needed to buy a gift for a friend whose birthday was on Monday. I opened the Amazon app, picked out the perfect gift, got to the checkout cart, and it said that the gift would be arriving on Tuesday. I panicked. That was too late! I had procrastinated and was hoping Prime would come through for me. I was out of luck, but I ordered anyway and figured I would just have to give it to him late. Around three o'clock the next afternoon, I heard a knock on the door. There on my doormat was a package. I was flustered. Did someone else in the family order something? I looked on the box and it had my name on it. To my surprise, it was my friend's gift!! The Amazon confirmation said it would be delivered Tuesday, but it was in my hands in one day.

I believe that God has some deliveries for you that are going to come sooner than you think. All the circumstances, reports, other people, and confirmations may say it's going to take years for your dream to come to pass, to get out of debt, or meet the right person. I'm encouraging you to stir up your faith and get ready. I hear the knock on your door. God has some things with your name on it. You are about to see that miracle, that promise or breakthrough you've been praying for. An unexpected delivery is coming to the door of your life.

Faith is the currency of Heaven. Faith is what unlocks Heaven and all of God's promises. If we want to see God's hand move in our lives, we have to release our faith. Our needs don't release God's favor, His promises, or the victory that's stored up for us. Faith does. It's not about the size of our faith (Jesus put that to rest with the whole mustard seed/moving mountains thing). It's about the size of the *object* of our faith. When you release your faith to Jesus, the One who watches over His Word and who is anxious to perform it goes to work (Jeremiah 1:12). He sets miracles in motion in your life.

> It's not about the size of our faith. It's about the size of the *object* of our faith.

We see this so clearly in the life of Daniel. In Daniel 9, he had prayed and released his faith. While he was still praying, an angel came with the answer and said, "Daniel, I have now come to give you insight and understanding. As soon as you began to pray, a word went out, which I have come to tell you, for you are highly esteemed" (Daniel 9:22–23 NIV). Just as with Daniel, the moment you pray, God releases the answer. He releases the healing, the promotion, the deliverance. It's already en route. Now do your part and declare, "Lord, thank You that it's on the way. I know You're faithful to Your Word and anxious to perform it. You say that as I pray, the tide of the battle begins to turn." I believe things are turning, being released and set in motion in your life, and I believe it's going to happen sooner than expected.

A Miracle Is at the Door

In Acts 12, Peter was in prison awaiting trial. He was not just in a holding cell; he was in maximum security bound with two chains and sixteen guards assigned to him. It didn't look good for him. The Bible says something else was happening while Peter was asleep in prison. Across town, behind closed doors, a group of believers had gathered at Mary's house and were praying for Peter. They knew it was a very serious situation. The apostle James had been put to death previously. Peter was just a few hours away from possibly losing his life, so they gathered and released their faith for him. As they were praying, an angel of the Lord showed up in Peter's cell and proceeded to break chains, open cell doors, and set him free. It was a miraculous rescue. A holy heist took place!

Peter walked out of the prison, realized that what had just happened was real and not a dream, then walked toward the only place he thought he'd be safe. He went to the very place where the believers were praying for him and knocked on the door. Think about it. The believers were praying for Peter's freedom, and little did they know that he was standing at the door. The answer to their prayers was knocking on their door!! Their faith, not just their need, put a miracle in motion. As they released their faith, God released the miracle.

There are things in your life that you're hoping will come, will change, will shift. When you release your faith concerning these things, make no mistake about it—God moves. No chain, no person, no wall can keep your promise from getting to you. It's just a matter of time before it gets to the door of your life. Be encouraged that while you're praying for your healing, healing is already en route. When you're praying for the breakthrough, the angel has already loosed the chains. When you're praying for a family member who's off course, God has already set the miracle in motion.

What's funny is that the believers who were praying for Peter couldn't believe Peter was actually at the door. Peter knocked on the outer entrance and said, "Hey, it's Pete. Let me in. Hurry! I don't want them to see me!" A lady named Rhoda came to the door, heard Peter's voice, and was so overjoyed that she ran back in and didn't even open the door. When she told everyone that Peter was at the door, they said, "Rhoda, what are you smokin'? That's impossible. Peter is chained in the prison. You must be seeing things. Calm down." The whole time Peter was knocking at the door and thinking, *Come on! I'm the answer to your prayer. I'm the miracle you are believing for. At least let me in.* It was a delivery that they didn't see coming. It wasn't just that God answered; it was that it happened sooner than they thought.

> No chain, no person, no wall can keep your promise from getting to you.

Sometimes God works over a long period of time. There are other times when God does something suddenly. When He does, you cannot explain it and you cannot take credit for it. It's just a God delivery! A work of His hand. It's incomprehensible and it's a powerful testimony to those around you.

Undeserved Miracles

A friend of mine named Marvin had given his life to Christ, but he still battled with depression and anxiety. In March, he started to experience severe anxiety attacks that seriously impacted his sleeping and eating habits. He lost thirty pounds in one month, and his condition finally led him to admit himself into the emergency room. He told me that even though he felt overwhelmed, he felt safe there. Marvin said that the funny thing about the emergency room is that while you are there, they do a great job of letting you forget that you have to pay for treatment. But they do an incredible job of *reminding* you that you have to pay for that treatment once you are released. Over the span of a week, he watched bill after bill come in and add up to over $20,000 in medical charges.

Marvin started to believe that God had abandoned him. Then Easter Sunday came around, and he felt compelled to come to Lakewood. The message he heard was to believe that God is up to something even when you don't see anything changing. He said that day he stirred up his faith and trusted God again. Two days later, someone from the HR department at his company knocked on his office door and delivered the news that he was eligible for full health benefits. Not only that, but they were backdating his policy to the beginning of March! That meant that nearly all of his ER bills were covered. God turned $20,000 of debt into $1,500 in less than five minutes. What happened? He received a knock on his door. God delivered a miracle sooner than expected. God had his back. Marvin told me that he didn't feel worthy of this miracle because of the doubt he was battling. I told him what I'm telling you: God doesn't overlook your door because you make mistakes, have a past, or even at times doubt because you don't see anything happening. In fact, none of us ever deserves or can earn these sudden miracles. These deliveries happen, not because of our goodness, but as a display and expression of the goodness of God.

In Joshua 2, the Israelites were poised to cross the Jordan River. Joshua sent two spies to scout out the Promised Land and assess if they would be successful invading, especially the city of Jericho. The spies traveled into Jericho and needed to hide for their safety, so they approached a house that was owned by a prostitute named Rahab, knocked on the door, and asked if she would

> God doesn't overlook
> your door because
> you make mistakes,
> have a past, or even at
> times doubt because
> you don't see anything
> happening.

hide them. They vowed that if she helped them, they would keep her and her family safe and establish them when the Israelites took the land. Rahab courageously helped them, and they successfully returned to Joshua. After the Israelites defeated the city of Jericho, "Joshua spared Rahab the prostitute and her relatives who were with her in the house, because she had hidden the spies Joshua sent to Jericho. And she lives among the Israelites to this day" (Joshua 6:25 NLT).

This had been an unexpected and undeserving knock on the door of Rahab's life. She didn't earn this. It's safe to assume that she'd done things that she wasn't proud of on that very day. Then two men knocked on her door. Was she thinking, *Another client?* It's as though God set this moment up to say, "You may be at your worst, but I'm coming to be good to you. I'm delivering a miracle to your door. I want to spare your legacy. I'm choosing to reveal My goodness to you, and it's undeserved." This knock not only meant safety, but represented a new beginning. Not only would she be protected, but she married an Israelite and became the great-great-grandmother of David, whose lineage would bring us Jesus, the Savior of the world!

One knock at the door, one sudden undeserved delivery, can change the trajectory of your family. This is what God wants to do in your life. Sometimes the miracle comes when we least deserve it. You weren't praying for it. You didn't ask for it. God surprised you. He chose you in His goodness. Stop talking yourself out of your miracles. Stop talking yourself out of why your family can't overcome and be blessed. Stop talking yourself out of why you don't deserve it because of your past, your mistakes, or where you come from. If you are reading this and have faith in Jesus, you are a candidate for a miracle.

I encourage you to live your life by the door. In other words, live expecting God's goodness. Don't think, *Why me?* Instead, start thinking, *Why not me?* Don't allow your past, or your circumstances, or what people have said to distract or push you away from your promise. I hear some knocking on the doors of your life. Regardless of what you are currently seeing, stir up your faith to hear it—the financial miracle, the healing, the sudden deliverance from that addiction. You can live the dream, content and knowing what is supposed to be yours will come to you. You don't have to worry, strive, coerce, or manipulate to make it happen. You can rest knowing that God's favor and goodness are chasing you down.

Trusted with Favor

> Don't think, *Why me?* Instead, start thinking, *Why not me?*

It is clear that God's favor follows you. The question is: How are you stewarding that favor? What are you doing with it? As we saw with David and Joseph, favor follows you so you can be a blessing. You are favored so you can lift others and be an example and display of God's love and goodness. That is seen in Joseph's story when he was in command of Egypt and his brothers knelt before him in fear. "But Joseph replied, 'Don't be afraid of me. Am I God, that I can punish you? You intended to harm me, but God intended it all for good. He brought me to this position so I could save the lives of many people'" (Genesis 50:19–21 NIV).

God favored Joseph and brought him to that position, not just for his good but so he could serve and save others. God did not remove him and take him to a more comfortable or "Christian" place. He was promoted right there in Egypt to show those in that area the goodness of God! Favor is never just for you; it's so those around you can see and experience God's goodness as well.

> Favor is never just for you; it's so those around you can see and experience God's goodness as well.

You see the same in the story of Shadrach, Meshach, and Abednego in Daniel 3. These three Hebrew men refused to compromise while they were exiles in Babylon. They refused to bow and worship the king's idol. As a result, they were thrown into a fiery furnace. The Bible says that when King Nebuchadnezzar looked in the door of the furnace, there was a fourth man standing with them in the fire, one "like the Son of God" (Daniel 3:25 NKJV). Favor doesn't always keep you from the fire. Favor will sometimes follow you into it and protect you! The three men walked out untouched by the flames. They didn't even smell like smoke! Following the fiery rescue, King Nebuchadnezzar was so astonished by what happened that he promoted the three men to even greater positions of influence *in* Babylon. What happened? They were favored to make a lasting impact.

Let me ask you a question. What are you doing with your favor? Regardless of the environment or position you find yourself in, are you stewarding your influence to be good to others? As children of God, we are entrusted with favor. You are favored to make an impact, to make a difference in the lives of others around you. Steward it wisely and be good to people.

This is what livin' the dream is all about. It's about encouraging and giving to others! You can build others up, knowing that God is taking care of you. You can choose to be good to others, knowing God is going to continue to be good to you. In other words, act like you know and believe that Heaven has your back!

CHAPTER NINE

YOU HAVE NOTHING TO PROVE

Be Comfortable in Your Own Skin

One time when I was speaking at Lakewood, I started my message by holding up a new, crisp hundred-dollar bill, then I asked how much it was worth. The crowd yelled back, "One hundred dollars!" I then slowly creased and crumpled the bill in my hand and said that the bill was ugly, crumpled, and not good anymore. I held up the wad of paper and asked again, "How much is it worth now?" Again, the Lakewood family yelled, "One hundred dollars!" I dropped the crumpled bill on the stage, stepped on it, and dragged it around with my foot, picking up whatever residue might be lying there. I picked up the bill and asked a final time,

"How much now?" Again, "One hundred dollars!" Then I asked, "I wonder if there's anyone here who would still take this bill after all it's been through. Anyone still want it?" Of course, hands flew up everywhere. I called a college student to come up on the stage. She was excited and ran up to join me. I looked at her and asked, "Are you sure you want this? It's dirty, crumpled, worn-out, been through

> Your value is based solely on the fact that you are a child of God.

a lot." Without hesitation, she said, "Absolutely," took the bill, and walked happily back to her seat.

Despite what that bill had been through, how tattered and dirty it was, or what people said about it, its value had not changed. The same is true about you and your life. It doesn't matter what you've been through, the mistakes you've made, what you're currently battling, or what people have said about you—your value and worth have not changed. People can't change your value, and neither can you. Your value is based solely on the fact that you are a child of God. How someone treats you doesn't change your value. Mistakes you've made don't decrease your value. That's what you did. That's not who you are. You can buy a bigger house, drive an expensive car, or get the title you've always wanted, but that doesn't increase your value. You can increase your net worth, but not your self-worth. You may be a stay-at-home mom raising your children and not appear as important as the CEO of the company you left, but the two of you have the same value. Your value is not based on what you do, where you live, or who you know. Those things can change. Your value comes from your Creator. God breathed His life into you.

YOU HAVE NOTHING TO PROVE

Performance, Possessions, and Popularity

Fulfilling your purpose for your generation is directly connected to you consistently rediscovering your value and uniqueness. Now, this gets difficult when we see everyone else's highlight reel on social media, and the pressure builds to match other people's highlights. It becomes easy to feel less-than. Your body isn't good enough, your wardrobe isn't trendy enough, and your house isn't Pottery Barn enough. Over time, it's easy to feel as though *you* aren't enough. The enemy will use all kinds of things to try to devalue you. He will work overtime trying to get you to compare your life to somebody else's, trying to get you to think that you will feel good about yourself when you catch up to them, when you live in a certain neighborhood, or when you perform perfectly. Then you'll finally be valuable. But nothing you achieve, overcome, or possess can make you more valuable than you are right now.

> Nothing you achieve, overcome, or possess can make you more valuable than you are right now.

In Luke 4, the enemy tried this on Jesus through the three temptations in the desert. Jesus had been out in the wilderness, where for forty days He had been tempted and not eaten any food. The enemy came to Jesus and said, "If you are the Son of God, tell this stone to become bread" (v. 3 NIV). The devil was trying to get Jesus to base His value on His performance. He was saying, "If You turn these stones into bread, You can prove You are the Son of God. You can feel good about Yourself." Jesus wouldn't do it. He said, "Man shall not live on bread alone" (v. 4 NIV). He was saying, in effect, "I don't have to do anything to prove who I am. I don't have to *perform* to feel good about Myself. I know who I am."

The enemy couldn't deceive Jesus into shifting His value into being performance-based, so he tried possession-based. He took Jesus to a high place, showed Him all the kingdoms of the world, and said, "You can possess all the authority and splendor if You will just bow down and worship me." Jesus said, "No, thanks. I don't need possessions or worldly authority to prove My value. I don't have to have what you think is important to feel good about who I am."

Possession-based appeal didn't work. Performance-based temptation didn't work. So the enemy tried one final approach: popularity. He took Jesus to the highest place of the temple, which would have been very crowded below, and he said, "If you are the Son of God, throw yourself down from here. For it is written: 'He will command his angels concerning you to guard you carefully'" (vv. 9–10 NIV). He was trying to get Jesus to show off. He'd gain instant popularity if He wowed the crowd. He'd get a thousand likes and comments in the feed and a million views on YouTube. Jesus said, "No, I don't need people's applause to feel valuable. I know who I am. I'm the Son of the living God."

> You don't have to prove anything to anyone to feel valued.

What's interesting is that the timing of this temptation immediately followed Jesus' baptism. The Father had just spoken from Heaven and said, "This is my Son, whom I love; with him I am well pleased" (Matthew 3:17 NIV). Jesus was just about to step into His ministry, into revealing His love and power in various ways. You were also designed to step into your world knowing your worth, not looking for the world to tell you what you are worth. It's very freeing when you realize you don't have to prove anything to anyone to feel valued. It's very powerful when you become aware of who you are and whose you are.

One of a Kind

You haven't been mass-produced on an assembly line. You have been carefully created. Look at your thumbprint and notice the details. Your thumbprint is unique to you. No one else on this planet has the same fingerprint as you.

That's only the beginning of how unique you are. Depending on where you are reading this, feel free to yell "Hey!" Go ahead and give it a shout. Now, you may not think much of that sound, but it's significant. There isn't another person among the eight billion on this planet who has the same exact sound as you. Perhaps you're like me and you can't carry a tune, but that doesn't mean that your voice isn't significant.

> When God made you, He broke the mold. You are the first time you've ever happened!

While putting one foot in front of another might seem like a simple act, researchers confirm that we all have our own unique swagger, our own strut. Each of us has tiny bounces and ways of swinging our legs that are unique.

What am I saying? When God made you, He broke the mold. You are the first time you've ever happened, and you will never happen again! You are a one-off! A one in a billion.

Too often we so easily forget about our own significance and uniqueness, which leaves us prone to comparing ourselves and trying to keep up with people who have an entirely different calling and purpose for their lives.

I was recently working out at a gym that some good friends had just opened in Houston. It was a highly effective group-format training. This was one of my first times at the gym, and it happened to be one of the hottest days of the summer. When I walked in that day, I looked at the schedule on the wall and noticed that pushing sleds was part of the agenda. Men and women separated into two lines on the turf, and I found myself second in our line. One at a time, each man pushed the sled down the turf about twenty yards and back. After each of us went through each set, the first guy could choose to add weight, and then the guys after him had the choice to either take it off, put more weight on, or leave it. During the first three sets, no one changed the weight, and I was feeling pretty good. The fourth set came around and the guy before me looked at the sled, looked at the rest of us, and added weight. He pushed the sled down and back with ease, and stopped it right in front of me. Now I had to decide what I was going to do. I was feeling tired but all eyes were on me. I left the additional weight on for that fourth set and pushed the sled down and back with all I had. I was exhausted, but I was able to leave that station and move to the next one. However, as soon as I hit the next station, I felt a huge wave of nausea come over me. The decision I'd made earlier had caught up to me. I ran out of the gym and found a spot on the side of the building and lost my lunch. I was so embarrassed and walked back in looking white as a ghost. Let's just say I struggled to make it through the rest of the workout.

That day I got caught up trying to push a weight I wasn't designed for or strong enough to push. Trying to keep up with someone else set me back, and I wasn't able to function at my best. My question is: Who are you trying to keep up with? I wonder how many of us are adding emotional weight to our lives trying

to be someone or something that we're
not. Are you getting caught up in social
media comparing yourself to others?
Are you measuring who you are and
what you have to those around you? I'm
not saying you shouldn't honor, respect,
and learn from other people. But I am

> Are you measuring
> who you are and
> what you have to
> those around you?

saying that comparing can quickly tempt you to forget about your
value, uniqueness, and the purpose God has designed just for you.

Step Out of Comparison

God beckons you out of comparison and into your own unique
calling, into what He designed you to be. First Samuel 16 presents
an excellent example of this. While King Saul ruled over Israel,
the prophet Samuel was directed by God to go to the house of
Jesse with a plan to anoint the next king of Israel. Jesse brought
seven of his sons out, but not the youngest, David. Samuel looked
at the sons and asked if there were any sons missing. Jesse said yes,
but that David was out in the field taking care of the sheep. When
David was brought in, to everyone's surprise, Samuel took one
look at him and anointed David to be king.

Here's what we discover. Jesse didn't think that David had
what it took. Sometimes the people closest to you can't see what's
inside you. Even David's own father discounted him. People may
leave you out, but God will make sure your purpose finds you.
I know it hurts when people don't see your value, but you don't
need anyone's approval to reach your destiny.

Samuel anointed David to be the next king, but nothing
changed. David went back to tending the sheep, with a king's
anointing. But one day David was asked to deliver a provision of

food to his brothers who were on the front lines of battle with the Philistines. David discovered that the giant Goliath was taunting and intimidating the Israelites, and it stirred up his spirit. He was brought before King Saul and asked for permission to fight Goliath. Given David's size and complete lack of military training and experience, Saul tried unsuccessfully to talk him out of it, but suggested that David wear his armor, thinking that David must have a coat of armor, helmet, and sword. The temptation for David, as it is for you and me, was to try to put something on that wasn't designed for him. David tried Saul's armor on but quickly

> You don't need anyone's approval to reach your destiny.

realized that it was too big for him and would only impede him. In the face of serious temptation, David courageously declined. He took his staff, five smooth stones, and the sling he had mastered while protecting his sheep. He brought stones to a sword fight, and guess what happened? He won with a single shot, and the Israelites went on to victory.

Despite his father's lack of approval and others trying to get him to do it their way, David knew his value. He knew God had given him his own unique abilities. David knew who and whose he was.

Throughout your life, when you don't realize your value, you will be tempted to put on someone else's armor. It might be someone else's pace of living, someone else's house or car, someone else's position, or someone else's mind-set. Do you know who wrote, "I am fearfully and wonderfully made" (Psalm 139:14 NIV)? David did. In the face of pressure and jealousy, he knew who he was. You have to believe that what God has given you is enough. As with David, the more you recognize where your value comes from, and that you have unique abilities and experience that no one else does, that's when your God opportunities will come to you!

Keep Your Eyes on Your Own Lane

You can be walking in God's best. You can be in your own lane winning your own race, but then you see someone else's life and influence and begin to compare. When you do, you immediately lose sight of your lane and stray off, eventually limiting and delaying God's best for your life.

Two of my college years I lived with my mom and step father. One day while I was on my way home, my mom asked me to stop at the store for her, but instead of going right to the store, I took the long way there so I could drive by a friend's house to see what he was doing. As I approached the house, a group of my friends were all out front. I got all excited, leaned out the window, and started doing my best Chris Farley impersonation, waving and yelling obnoxiously. If you know me, you know that Farley is one of my favorite comedic actors of all time. I can almost quote *Tommy Boy* and *Black Sheep* line for line. My friends saw me coming from way off, hanging out the window and yelling. As I sped toward the house, their smiles suddenly changed to looks of concern. Instead of waving back, they started pointing in front of me. I looked up and a pizza delivery car had stopped twenty feet in front of me at the intersection and was waiting to turn. I hit the brakes too late and skidded right into the car's rear end. Thank God, my airbags deployed and I wasn't injured. The delivery car barely had a scratch, and the driver was fine, but my car was totaled, and pizza was everywhere. My friends were laughing hysterically, and I wasn't. This is what happens when you take your eyes off your lane and fail to see what's in front of you. I was trying so hard to impress my friends, and it set me back big time. I spent most of that summer trying to make enough money to buy my next car.

> Are you living your life striving for the approval of others?

Are you living your life striving for the approval of others? Maybe you haven't rear-ended a pizza delivery car, but you could be missing out on all that God is doing in your lane because you are too distracted looking at someone else's lane. I compare it to the same thing that occurs every time there's a major car accident and people slow down on the other side of the highway just to see what's happening. Then, not only is the lane the accident happened in congested, but the lane going the opposite direction becomes jammed as well and often it leads to another accident. It's very frustrating, and we're all guilty of gawking at the other lane. The crazy thing is, the traffic jam is not due to an accident; it's due to people looking at the other lanes!!

I wonder what's being held up in your life because you are distracted by someone who's in another lane. Are you comparing? Scrolling? So caught up in other people's stories that you are missing the opportunity to create your own?

Keep Your Eyes on Your Mug

A friend of mine told me that you will never know your cup is overflowing when you have your eyes on someone else's mug. I know how true this is. It's easy to discount what I have in my life when I'm constantly watching and comparing my life to what other people have. God has given us a cup that's overflowing with blessings, value, and promise. We should never discount it.

David could sling a rock. That may not sound very impressive and may not make for the coolest profile pic, but God used that slingshot to get him on the throne. Imagine if David had focused on what King Saul had and tried to be like Saul and didn't think what he had was significant. His life would have looked different.

Remember when Jesus fed the five thousand? Before that happened, He asked the disciples for whatever they had. They looked around and found a boy who had five loaves of bread and two fish. If we go back even further, and use our imagination, that boy had a mom who woke up early that day and packed that lunch for him. When she did, I'm sure it seemed insignificant and ordinary. It wasn't Instagrammable. But what she made was multiplied and used in blessing thousands. Imagine if that mom had been so caught up in social media that day and so lost in comparison that she forgot to make that lunch. Imagine her thinking, *This isn't important. Other moms are starting businesses, doing big things, and I'm stuck at home making lunches.* It seemed ordinary, but what she made turned into a miracle.

Today, you may not have all you want, but you have to realize that what you have is enough. Change your perspective on what you have.

I read a story about a man who spent his life barely getting by and died in abject poverty. After the funeral, some of his family members went to his run-down apartment to gather his belongings. They took a few things they wanted and decided to arrange a garage sale to get rid of his leftover belongings, including an old painting he had had for many years. Someone at the sale bought the painting and took it to an art expert to learn more about it. It turned out that it was an original painting from a renowned artist in the 1800s whose artwork was highly sought after. That painting was eventually put up for sale at an art auction and sold for three million dollars.

The man had lived a destitute life because he didn't know what he possessed. As with this man, you can be missing out on the life God designed for you because you don't realize the value that you carry and possess. The painting didn't look like much to the man's family members, so they sold it for next to nothing. What made this painting valuable wasn't who owned it or where it was located. What gave it immense value was who painted it. Because of who your Maker is, you are valuable. You have been carefully created by the Master Painter. You are full of purpose, destiny, and potential. You have the fingerprints of God all over you. You are a child of the Most High God. That is who you are, that is whose you are, and that is what you carry. The best thing you can give your future is a healthy, content, unashamed you.

> The best thing you can give your future is a healthy, content, unashamed you.

Change Spoons

Making chocolate milk can change your life.

One day my son, Denver, wanted chocolate milk. So I poured some Nesquik chocolate syrup in the bottom of a large glass and filled it with milk. Denver grabbed a spoon and stirred it, but his spoon couldn't reach the bottom where the syrup was. He picked the glass up and tried the milk, which was not the rich flavor he was hoping for. I told him he needed a longer spoon that could reach the space at the bottom. He grabbed a large wooden spoon and gave it another try. This time when he tried it, it was the chocolate milk of his dreams. What happened? He discovered something that could reach the space at the bottom of the glass.

I like to think of the glass of milk as our heart and soul, and there's a place in the bottom of our life where God put our value. The short spoon is man's approval and attention. It's good, and it feels great in the moment, but it cannot fully reach the bottom of our longing to be valued. It can never satisfy the deep need in our heart. Over time, the spoons change, the acclaim and ovations change. We get the titles, the promotion, the applause, and we get the car and the house and stuff. And they all stir us up and make us feel good for a while. But there's still that inner place where those things cannot reach, and we're left still feeling empty, unfulfilled, and unsatisfied. We can either continue to look to other people (short spoons) to applaud our efforts and cheer us on, or we can come to the realization that Someone is already giving us a standing ovation (big spoon). Whether we believe it or not, whether we feel it or not, God accepts, affirms, and delights in us. He sees who you are, and He claps. He is the only one who can satisfy your soul, who can meet your deep need for validation and acceptance. You can live your whole life seeking and living for other people's approval, hoping those spoons somehow stir up your value. Or you can live knowing and believing the truth that God loves and approves of you. You can live as the person you were designed to be, fully confident in who you are in Jesus.

You Have Nothing to Prove

In John 7, Jesus "did not want to go about Judea because the Jewish leaders there were looking for a way to kill him. But when the Jewish Festival of Tabernacles was near, Jesus' brothers said to him, 'Leave Galilee and go to Judea, so that your disciples there may see the works you do. No one who wants to become a public figure acts in secret. Since you are doing these things, show yourself to the world.' For even his own brothers did not believe in him. Therefore Jesus told them, '…You go to the festival. I am not going up to this festival, because my time has not yet fully come.' After he had said this, he stayed in Galilee" (vv. 1–9 NIV).

Even Jesus' brothers didn't believe He was who He said He was. They wanted Him to prove who He was, not just to those in Judea, but to themselves. It was what they expected He would do, because anytime there is unbelief about our lives, we will naturally try to perform to prove something. Many of us don't believe we're valuable; we can't see or have forgotten our strengths and uniqueness. You may secretly feel that you have so much less to offer than you try to portray. Even when people pay you compliments, you may think, *Oh, you don't see who I really am.* We all struggle with this and try to perform to measure up. We overcompensate because we don't feel that we're enough. Because we don't believe we are unique, special, and valuable, we have to prove that we're a good dad or mom, or that we're intelligent, or that we have a significant position. We have to post about it and prove to others that we're enough.

Jesus was going to Judea, but it would be in His time, and He had nothing to prove. He purposefully stayed away from Judea for the moment because He was not going to give the Jewish leaders an opportunity to kill Him before His time had come. He refused to give in to the temptation to prove Himself to his family or anyone else. He was saying, "I know who I am and the power I possess. I don't need to prove it to other people, and I won't move forward before the right time."

Let me ask you: Whom or what do you need to purposefully stay away from? Whom do you need to purposefully stop comparing yourself to, or proving who you are to, or keeping up with? Are you waiting for God's timing to shape you into the person He wants you to be? You are already approved and valued by God; therefore, you have nothing to prove to anyone. God leads an ovation in Heaven over your life today. It's not because you are a scholar, or lead the company in sales, or because you are verified on Instagram. No, it's simply because you are His child. You don't have to try to impress Him or other people. Just be who He's created you to be, knowing where your worth and value come from and refusing to compare yourself with or perform for others.

> God leads an ovation in Heaven over your life today.

If you do this, I believe and declare you're going to live free, confident, secure, and become the masterpiece that God created you to be. You are not who the world and social media and other people say you are. You are who God says you are. You are a victor, His beloved, wonderfully made, and because of Jesus, you are enough and you have nothing to prove. You can say, "I'm livin' the dream because I know my worth and value. I'm not living for the approval of people. God already approves of me!"

CHAPTER TEN

LIVE WITHIN THE MARGINS

Embrace Your God-Given Limits

'Ve never been a fan of essays. Maybe you're like me and tend to procrastinate until a few days before the five-page essay is due. So you try to get by with a 30-point font instead of the required 12. To reach the required page limit, you might triple-space between lines instead of the required double-space. If you are *really* good, you increase the margins, causing the words to fill more of the pages, which makes the essay appear longer than it really is. My teachers never let me get by with these tricks, even the incorrect margins.

Most documents, books, magazines, and anything that gets published have appropriate margins for two reasons. Suitable margins help the reader see words clearly. Margins are also created for reflection or space for the reader to write in. These created boundaries allow people to respond to what is written or communicated. In other words, the boundaries and margins are intentional. Think about your life for a moment. Does it have margins? Chances are, if you are like me, it's easy to succumb to the temptation to push our lives beyond what we're designed to do and max out "our space." We're always pushing beyond the appropriate edge. We're

> One of the reasons many of us are not livin' the dream is that we're doing way more than God has called us to do.

maxing out emotionally and physically. We're consistently pushing beyond what we can handle, so we're always tired, emotionally fatigued, and lacking joy. Is that you? Are you saying no to things, or are you saying yes to every opportunity, every relationship, every social activity, and discovering the hard way that you are overcommitting?

I've discovered that one of the reasons many of us are not livin' the dream is that we're doing way more than God has called us to do. We're pushing beyond our God-given limits, trying to do too much with too little. We are spinning more plates than we were designed to spin. And we have no margins, no boundaries set up to help us refrain from the temptation to live on overload.

In Psalm 119, the psalmist makes it clear that he's learned that he must live his life within the constraints of God's precepts and commands. He has learned that he cannot do it all or whatever he wants, that God has created him with limits that must be recognized and honored. We all have physical limits. You can't go six months without food, no matter how hard you try. We all have emotional limits. You can only give so much to others, you can only carry so much drama, and you can only carry and process so many problems. We all have mental limits. You can only process a certain amount of information. We all have time limits. You're never going to have more than twenty-four hours in a day, and you have to sleep during some of that time. God created you with limits because He loves you and He wants to work with you, to partner with you. These limits are naturally designed so we can depend on God when we reach those limits.

> You can be all God designed you to be, but you cannot be whatever you want to be.

The problem is that we live in a society that says, "You can do it all, you can have it all, and you can be whatever you want." That sounds really good, really positive, but that isn't true. You can be all God designed you to be, but you cannot be whatever you want to be. God has a unique plan for each of us to accomplish, and it's within our limits. To become all God created you to be and reach your full potential, you have to realize that your life has to have margins. You have to embrace the limits of your ability, while trusting God's limitless ability to make up the difference.

What am I saying? Sometimes it takes more strength and faith to create margins in our life and trust God to do what you haven't been graced to do. Oftentimes, reaching your destiny is as much about possessing the strength and faith to say no as it is to say yes.

In 1989, the *Exxon Valdez* oil supertanker struck a reef just off the coast of Alaska. The crash resulted in the second largest oil spill in US history. Eleven million gallons of crude oil spilled into the ocean. Scientists estimated that 250,000 sea birds, 3,000 otters, 300 seals, and 250 bald eagles died due to the accident. This environmental tragedy created a serious compromise to human and animal life in that region. Investigators reported the primary reason for this accident was severe fatigue among the crew and the captain. The report revealed that the captain and the crew had worked around the clock for weeks with no physical and mental rest. In other words, they had no margins. They were way past maxing out. As a result, the ship's valuable content, designed to help propel and support life, was lost and ended up destroying life.

> Oftentimes, reaching your destiny is as much about possessing the strength and faith to say no as it is to say yes.

Friend, you are carrying precious, valuable "cargo." If you aren't careful, if you don't learn that you have limits and that you need to create margins in your life, you can put the God-given cargo inside you at risk.

Physical and emotional fatigue is one of the greatest causes of compromise in our society. Fatigue distorts our perception of who we are, how valuable we are, and what we carry. Fatigue taints our ability to make wise decisions. Fatigue impacts how we love and treat those around us. What I'm saying is that we need to be healthy. Reaching your destiny requires that you make the decision to set some margins and boundaries in your life.

Blessings in the Boundaries

In Exodus 18, Moses had led the Israelites out of slavery and into the wilderness on the way to the Promised Land. He was their leader, and they were relying heavily on him to give them the direction and care they needed. Moses had a purpose, and his purpose was directly connected to the success of the Israelites.

In this text, we discover that Moses was working from morning until evening, seeing the people, one after another, hearing their complaints and problems and rendering judgment when there were disputes. It's clear he was a leader who had no margins. He had not set boundaries, so he was working overtime and exhausting himself on small matters that would keep him from providing leadership on the really important matters. Then his father-in-law, Jethro, observed what was happening. Perhaps his daughter complained about her husband working too much, then coming home at night stressed out, emotionally and physically exhausted and never fully present. Either way, Jethro saw firsthand what Moses was doing for the people.

> Are you trying to be everything for everyone?

The key here is that Moses was running on empty while he was doing a good thing. He was maxing out while doing a great thing. He was helping people. He was counseling, advising, solving problems, inspiring, and encouraging. This wasn't a question of whether he was leading. This was about *how* Moses was leading. Jethro asked Moses, "Why are you doing all of this alone? The people have been standing here all day to get your help. This isn't good! You are going to wear yourself out and the people, too! This job is too heavy a burden for you to handle all by yourself." In other words, he was saying, "Moses, recognize that you have limits. You need to create some margins. You need to set some boundaries in your life—for you, for your family, and catch this, for *the people* to prosper."

Moses' life had transitioned and changed, but his margins had not. He entered a new season of leadership, but he was continuing to try to lead in an old way. Pharaoh had been the enemy of Moses; now it was his margins. Pharaoh tried to destroy him; now his lack of margins was about to. Pharaoh was no longer Moses' enemy; Moses was. Jethro advised Moses to empower honest, capable judges to serve the people and handle the smaller cases, and if anything major or serious emerged, they could bring it to him. Moses took his advice, delegated and empowered, and guess what happened? He won, his family won, and the people experienced peace and flourished. You know what else? Some strong leaders stepped up and felt the satisfaction of helping people and fulfilling their purpose. Gifts in others came alive. All of this, because one man created some boundaries.

Have you taken time lately to assess your margins? Have you changed jobs, stepped into a new season, but you're working with old margins? Are you trying to be everything for everyone? As with Moses, it's time to realize that you can't do it all. It's time to create some margins, to empower some people, and release your faith to God for the rest. Maybe it's time you exercise your faith by saying no to what no longer is yours to do. There's blessing in boundaries.

When You Say Yes to Everything

Oftentimes the enemy fights your morality by fighting your margins. His attacks in some seasons aren't public and blatant. Sometimes they are simple assaults on your boundaries. One way is to keep you overly busy emotionally and physically, even with good things. He will attempt to bombard you with information, with needs, with things to get done, with people to impress. He'll get you going 100 miles an hour to a place of fatigue, getting you to a place where you miss deadlines. You'll be tempted to say yes to everything so you are not as focused, so your ideas aren't as sharp, so your family suffers, and so your department grows unstable because of it. It won't be the result of you doing too little; it will be your inability to say no and to set boundaries for yourself and those closest to you. The enemy thinks, *If I can tire them out, keeping them busy, they will be more susceptible to compromise and distraction, to possibly even missing their destiny.* What am I saying? The enemy will attempt to keep you busy, making sure you have no margins and your glass is spilling over.

> You will always have the temptation to take on more than you should.

You will always have the temptation to take on more than you should. Imagine that a drinking glass represents your life. Pour a little water in to represent the time commitments that are right for this season. Let's say you take on some extra work projects to impress the boss. Pour some water in. Then you start to regularly work overtime despite your spouse's objections. Pour some more in. Now you've added new clients. A little more water gets poured into the glass. You also expand your responsibilities in your position. More water. Then you start to work out at the gym three early mornings a week. Add some water, and your glass is nearly filled. Somebody talks you into coaching your child's sports team, and the additional water is at the brim. You've said yes to everything, and your glass is filled to the max.

The problem with a full glass of water is that when the inevitable bump in your life comes, the result is a spill, a mess, even losing what it contains. A maxed-out life can't handle interruptions, delays, or unexpected events...which always occur. The enemy will attempt to keep you so busy that every interruption or delay sends you into a complete tailspin because your life is too full. Your calendar and emotional health are not on the same page, and you find yourself yelling at your kids and spouse, reacting and not responding, cutting corners, and easily irritated.

Sean Collins is a great friend of mine. He has a nice fishing boat and was the first to take Denver and me out saltwater fishing. He's one of the most generous guys I know, always willing to give his time to serve and help others. One Saturday, my father-in-law was in town and wanted to go fishing. One call to Sean, and in no time we were loading the boat and setting off into the bay, looking for the first good redfish spot. Off in the distance, I saw what looked like a large ripple in the water. However, as we got closer, the size of it swelled. Before we knew it, we were twenty yards from a huge set of waves. Sean saw them and slammed the throttle back, bringing the boat to a dead stop. We were grasping whatever we could hold on to in order not to get thrown into the water. Then four or five massive waves rocked the boat up and down, with each wave sending the tip of the boat into the water and water into the boat. Thankfully, the set of waves passed and there was no damage to the boat or us. Sean looked at us and said, "Guys, you've just experienced a rogue wave." He told us that the cargo ships in the ship channel create them, and you have to be constantly watching for them when you are driving fast. Rogue waves can come out of nowhere and cause major problems, even capsize your boat.

Have you ever had a set of rogue waves interrupt your life? You didn't see them coming? You were on course, you had plans, then the unexpected hit and brought your life and plans to a stop. Perhaps it was a diagnosis from the doctor. An unexpected car failure. Your kids got sick. An economic downturn. When you're living your life at a frantic pace with no margins, a rogue wave can throw your world into chaos.

Here's what's crazy. Some of those interruptions might actually be God interruptions. When our glass is full, divine interruptions are often seen as obstacles instead of opportunities. You have to learn to assess your life and season and have the faith to say no to some things and create margins, so that when the unexpected happens, when change happens, you can respond appropriately. You'll have room and space to handle what comes your way. You can make great decisions and give that issue the proper attention it deserves.

Discover the Right Pace

> If Jesus set margins and lived within boundaries, how much more do we need them to fulfill our purpose?

What I find interesting is the pace at which Jesus lived His life. When you read and study Jesus' life, you discover that He often pulled away from the crowd to be alone. Sometimes His purpose was to get away to pray, and other times it was to simply get quiet and rest. Jesus showed us the need and the power of having margins in our lives. Why didn't He heal sick twenty-four seven? Why don't we see Him solving people's problems, feeding masses of hungry people, or teaching people day and night? There was no shortage of needs. But even Jesus didn't succumb to the temptation to do it all during His time on Earth.

We see the humanity of Jesus on display in the margins. He didn't live and lead at a frantic pace, with no margins. In fact, you never read that Jesus was in a rush. He was never hurrying or uptight. We see Jesus living purposefully, creating boundaries, and intentionally getting away to be rejuvenated. He rested. He enjoyed meals. He slept during storms. Every second of His life was strategic. Nothing was wasted. Every action and word had purpose. So you can say the margins were necessary for Jesus to fulfill His destiny.

If Jesus set margins and lived within boundaries, how much more do we need them to fulfill our purpose? How much better could you be as a parent, a spouse, or a coworker with some margins and boundaries in your life? Imagine what margins and boundaries could do to your stress level, fatigue level, anger, and even anxiety?

Miracles in the Margins

I had a schoolteacher who would make us draw in margins if our writing paper didn't have them. The reason was so she could write her encouragement, feed-back, and corrections in these margins. The margin was a strategic space for the teacher. Margins in your life aren't empty spaces of passivity and waste. You create margins so you can allow God to speak, encourage you, give you great ideas, and rejuvenate you. Boundaries aren't to push others away; boundaries are to help hold you together.

> Boundaries aren't to push others away; boundaries are to help hold you together.

Margins help provide clarity. Someone once told me never to make a critical decision when I am tired. Fatigue can alter our ability to properly assess and make good decisions. When I'm maxed out and fatigued, I don't see things clearly. My perspective is distorted. Margins allow us to gain clarity in our lives so we don't react to circumstances, but rather so we can properly respond. As the boundaries on a sheet of paper allow for assessment and proper adjustments, time set aside for quiet spaces allows you to process and gain the necessary clarity on your work, marriage, and challenges in life.

Margins foster creativity. Oftentimes when we're busy with the kids, busy with work, every weekend is slam packed, we just run according to old routines, methods, and ideas. When you establish some boundaries, you take time to turn life's volume down and get quiet. However that looks for you, it allows for God to give you new ideas. It might be new ways that your business can implement to perform better and be more innovative. You could get one idea that can catapult you five years ahead in your career. You might think of ways you can budget better at home or how you can take advantage of new technology. This is all because you created margins for the new. It's not because you took on more and got busier and ran faster, but because you had the courage to say no to some things, even good things, to put yourself in a position to get some great things.

Margins can build character. The lid on your life and potential is not your skills and gifts. Every day there are high-level CEOs, government leaders, business owners, and educators who get dismissed, not because they lacked competency, but because they lack character and integrity. Many fall short of reaching their full potential, not because they don't possess gifts, but because they didn't take the necessary time to build their character. Many of them would tell you that they were running at an unhealthy pace, relying on their gifts, but all the while neglecting the character development that exists in the margins of life. When you create space in your life for the Master Teacher to speak, the result is heart transformation and character development, and you can then sustain and handle the places God has planned to take you.

A margin is the space where you learn to say yes to Jesus' instruction and direction. It's where you say yes in response to

God and forgive others. You say yes to that idea for your company. Yes to the peace you need. Yes to being reminded of who you are. This space breeds contentment in who you are and where God has you in the season of life you are in. Set boundaries for yourself and watch what comes—not only will you be healthier, but you will begin to see God's limitless power unlocked and shown out in your life. You will experience more peace and make wiser decisions.

> When was the last time you set some boundaries so you could get quiet and listen?

Messages in the Margins

When was the last time you set some boundaries so you could get quiet and listen? When was the last time you turned off all the social media platforms, went for a walk in the park or sat in your backyard, and quieted your heart and soul? You know what happens when you do? You get familiar with God's voice. He may not give you long messages or thoughts. Many times, He just says:

"Trust Me."

"I love you."

"I'm proud of you."

"You're forgiven."

"Let it go."

"Take that step."

"I got you."

It's in this space, in the margins, where you allow Him to speak, to reveal Himself, and to develop who you are. It's the space you allow God to make deposits into your soul and encourage you. You don't have to live on chronic overload. Recognize the need to take care of what God has given you to steward. It's your precious purpose, talent, and gifts. Be courageous today and put some boundaries up and trust God's limitless ability. You will discover that there's a miracle in the margins for you. There are blessings in the boundaries. It's there where you can live the dream.

CHAPTER ELEVEN

BLESSINGS IN DISGUISE

Every Obstacle Brings an Opportunity

n chapter 7, I described some of the difficulties that Noah faced while building the ark. Recently, I saw something I'd never seen before while reading his story in Genesis 6–7. Noah had completed the ark, and the animals had settled into their temporary homes—all the feed and provisions were packed away. Noah and his family were all on board. However, we read in chapter 7 that the door of the ark remained opened until all the instructions from God were completed.

After 120 years of preparing the ark, the time had come for the flood. Water began to pour down as well as gush up from beneath the ground. It was time for the last critical move from Noah. The door of the ark needed to close. Was it a job for Noah? Was it his sons' job? Perhaps get a giraffe to stick its neck out there and pull it up? It started to really pour and suddenly the heavy door of the ark began to rise off the ground—not by the strength of a man, not by an animal, but by the unseen hand of God. Noah and family could hear the wooden door creak as it was lifted upward and shut tightly. "The Lord shut him in" (Genesis 7:16 NIV).

> We have to realize that closed doors are just as important as open doors.

After processing what had just happened, I imagine that Noah's family must have breathed a collective sigh of relief, feeling a sense of security, knowing that God had ensured the success of their undertaking. How did He ensure their future? Did you notice? By closing a door.

If Noah had been responsible for closing the door of the ark, would he have hesitated, thinking of all the people left outside? Perhaps God relieved Noah of the burden of shutting out the rest of humanity. For whatever reason, God shut the ark door Himself, and what a blessing that closed door was.

We like to think about how God opens doors in our lives. Open doors are naturally gratifying. We want to walk through those open doors, whether it's a promotion at work, a proposal of marriage, or a divine opportunity. Open doors are exciting, and when God is the One who opens them, they are a true blessing in our lives. But what about the blessing of a closed door? In Noah's situation, a closed door brought protection and preserved the human race and all of the animal life on the planet. We have to realize that closed doors are just as important as open doors. Fulfilling your purpose will come with some incredible open doors, but it will also come to pass by God allowing some strategic doors to close.

I've heard many agree with Garth Brooks and say, "I thank God for unanswered prayers." Although I understand what they are saying, I think the better way to say it is: "We should thank God when He answers our prayer in a *different* way than how we thought He was going to answer it." God always hears our prayers, and He always responds. But He may answer them differently than we think.

Closed on Purpose

One summer we were on a short vacation riding ATVs on a large piece of property. After we were done, my son, Denver, who was nine at the time, asked, "Dad, can I get a full-size four-wheeler? Pleeeeease. It would be so fun. Our neighbors have one. Come on, Dad. We can ride them together." He's a smart negotiator. Since he was only nine, though, I knew that it would be irresponsible to grant his request. It would put him in harm's way and at risk of a serious injury. As a loving father, I was glad he asked me. He knew I loved him and want the best for him, but since I knew the power of what he was asking for, and I knew what he was capable and incapable of in that season of his life, this was a closed door. I told him, "Not now, D. We will have to revisit this when you get a little older."

> Can I propose that perhaps the answer to that prayer or what you were hoping for is no because God has bigger and better plans in store for you?

I have a feeling that you may be facing a closed door, a no, a rejection of some form. You may have sent an application to graduate school or to a company and you got rejected. You were hoping for the promotion and you not only got a no, but they went a different route. You may have pursued someone and felt like that person was the one, but it didn't work out and they walked away. The door you were praying for closed. What you hoped for slammed shut. Can I propose that perhaps the answer to that prayer or what you were hoping for is no because God has bigger and better plans in store for you? Could God be protecting you from settling for less than His best? Could He be protecting and preventing something or someone from harming you?

As you look back over your life, I'm sure there are prayers you prayed that God didn't answer the way you wanted. You prayed that he or she would be the one, that the relationship would work out, but nothing developed and the two of you broke up. Years later, you see "the one's" true colors, and you realize it would have been the wrong relationship for you. You should be thanking God that the door shut. Or you prayed for a business to accept you for what looked like your dream job, but you didn't get a promised call-back. Then five months later you find out the company went bankrupt while you found a better position in a better company. Thank God for how He protected and rerouted you! He saved you. Looking back, can we thank Him for closing certain doors? Can we thank Him for prayers He didn't answer the way we wanted Him to? What would happen if we get to a place in our journey where we truly trust and believe that closed doors are just as blessed as open doors?

From Rejection to Redemption

In chapter 8, we looked at Joseph's story. We can see God guiding Joseph's life even through his mistreatment. He was betrayed and rejected by his own brothers, and he was faced with closed doors, unexpected detours, and overwhelming discouragement. In those moments, he had no idea why he was being rejected, but God knew that each of Joseph's painful steps was bringing him closer to his life's purpose. Rejection by men would ultimately put him in a position to offer redemption for an entire nation of people.

> I realize that every time I thought I was being rejected from something good, I was actually being redirected to something better.

I'm sure when Joseph first got a glimpse of his purpose through his dream as a young man, he did not imagine he would have to go through all he did to get there. But you could say that rejection protected and propelled him into his purpose. Maybe you are facing rejection from someone you love, from a job, or from a bank loan officer? It doesn't seem fair, but be encouraged—that closed door kept you from settling for something less than God's best. It may have been a good door, but it wasn't the best door.

As I look back over the course of my life, I realize that every time I thought I was being rejected from something good, I was actually being redirected to something better...to God's greater purpose! Often when a door closes, it's easy to "camp out" there, to stay hurt there and get bitter. We hold on to it when God has called us to move on. As we saw with Joseph, don't stay sitting outside the closed door, thinking about what could have happened. You have to move forward, knowing God has you in the palms of His hands, and He's going to use that closed door, that rejection, for a greater purpose.

Choose to Worship

We see how rejection can lead to a greater purpose in Genesis 29 with a woman named Leah. Leah was involved with her sister, Rachel, and Jacob in quite a dramatic love triangle. It began with Jacob going to work for his uncle Laban. He immediately noticed Laban's younger daughter, Rachel. The Bible says she had a lovely figure and was beautiful, and Jacob fell in love with her. So he decided to shoot his shot, went to Laban, and proposed to work seven years in return for Rachel's hand in marriage. Laban accepted the proposal, but when the seven years were over, he brought Leah to Jacob in the dark of their wedding night and tricked Jacob into thinking that she was Rachel (how Jacob didn't know this baffles me...perhaps too much wine). When he woke up the next morning, daylight revealed that it was Leah he'd married and not Rachel.

Jacob was furious! Leah was not his pick.

Now pause for a second. Jacob was obviously angry because he had worked seven years for the love of his life and then was deceived. But imagine how Leah must have felt. She was not chosen, not loved, and caught in the middle of her father's deceptive plan. She was innocent but rejected. She was the older daughter, hoping and planning and wishing that her wedding day would come, and when it did, it came in a way she never dreamed it would.

After figuring out what happened, Jacob married Rachel a week later, but only after he promised to work another seven years for Laban. So we have two sisters married to one man. There's jealousy, strife, and a whole lot of drama. This drama stemmed from this fact: "Jacob made love to Rachel also, and his love for Rachel was *greater* than his love for Leah" (Genesis 29:30 NIV).

Man, this was tough for Leah.

Leah would give birth to son after son with Jacob, and the names that Leah subsequently chose for her sons show her inward struggle, transformation, and journey. Genesis 29:32–34 (NIV) states, "Leah became pregnant and gave birth to a son. She named him Reuben, for she said, 'It is because the LORD has seen my misery. Surely my husband will love me now.' She conceived again, and when she gave birth to a son, she said, 'Because the LORD heard that I am not loved, he gave me this one, too.' So she named him Simeon. Again she conceived, and when she gave birth to a son, she said, 'Now at last my husband will become attached to me, because I have borne him three sons.' So he was named Levi." The name Reuben means "See a son," Simeon means "One who hears," and Levi means "Attached." We see her struggle to be loved, to be seen and heard and truly attached, hoping that having given Jacob three sons, so highly revered in their culture, would bring that. She's still reeling from rejection, hoping that having his sons would win him over and earn his love and companionship. But then something shifts in her when the fourth son is born. It says, "She conceived again, and when she gave birth to a son, she said, 'This time I will praise the LORD.' So she named him Judah" (Genesis 29:35 NIV). The name Judah means "Praise." We see a woman who was rejected and spent years fighting for security, fighting to be loved, fighting for her identity, and fighting to recover…

> God will turn the rejection in your life into a blessing.

…until something switches in this season of her life when Judah is born.

She reaches a point where she's no longer placing her identity in a man, in a position, and in her performance. In the wake of rejection and pain, she chose to worship and put her trust in the Lord.

She relinquished control of the difficult situation and in essence found her identity in Jesus. If only Leah could have fast-forwarded to the genealogy of Jesus in Matthew 1, she would have been amazed by what this change brought. As part of Jesus' lineage, it says, "Abraham was the father of Isaac, Isaac the father of Jacob, Jacob the father of Judah" (v. 2 NIV). If we jump all the way to verse 16, it says, "Joseph, the husband of Mary, and Mary was the mother of Jesus who is called the Messiah." Did you catch that? Jesus came from the line of Judah! Who gave birth to Judah? Leah. The wife whom Jacob never even wanted. The Savior of the world was born out of the rejection of Leah, who was unloved by Jacob.

Are you feeling rejected today? Feeling like a failure? Has a door closed on you? I'm here to tell you that out of your rejection, God is going to bring forth something powerful. As we see with Leah, God can turn the rejection in your life into a blessing. Yes, thank God for the open doors, but thank Him for the closed doors as well. That's difficult and requires faith. But it's that faith that produces something powerful. It's your faith that moves God to open the better doors He has in store for you.

Focus More on Who

Let me help you with a simple, practical idea. Usually when we're faced with a closed door, our natural reaction is to ask, "How?"

"How did this happen?"

"How am I going to meet the right one now?"

"How will I pay my bills?"

"How am I going to get well?"

"How am I going to get through school?"

"How am I going to recover?"

We get stuck thinking about the how.

I want to encourage you to Move the *W.* Move from HO*W* to *W*HO. Focus less on how it's going to happen, how you will get there, meet the right person, or make the payments, and focus more on *W*ho. Who is your healer? Who can provide for you? Who is in control of your destiny? Who can set miracles in motion in your life? The enemy will do his best to pressure you to figure it out, assume control, and carry the weight. But he didn't write your story; God did. God is the author and the finisher of your faith, so look to Him to provide for you at the right time. He will bring your spouse, bring you opportunities, and open doors in His timing. So put the *W* in the right place. You can win despite what appears to be a loss. This is what God planned when He says, "All things work together for good for those who love God" (Romans 8:28 NKJV). Stay in faith. God is turning your rejection into a blessing.

> I want to encourage you have to Move the *W.* Move from HO*W* to *W*HO.

Look Again

I love white elephant gift exchanges. Everyone brings a gift within a set price limit. The wrapped gifts are all placed in the middle of the room, and then you draw numbers to see who gets to pick first. What happens next is awesome. The first person scans the gifts—some small, some large, some in beautiful wrapping paper, some thrown in a bag, others primitively duct-taped in cardboard. The fun part is the way each person makes their choice. You base it on how it looks—the size, how it sits, how it's wrapped. You try your best to size up the gifts because it's against the rules to pick it up. A beautifully wrapped gift may hold a used children's book, a Shake Weight, or a Chia Pet. I once picked a gift that had a live fish in it! Maybe you've lucked out and picked the worst-wrapped gift and it turned out to be a gift card. That's usually what happens.

I wonder how many answered prayers, promises, provisions, and God opportunities we miss because they don't look like what we imagine. They are not "wrapped" how we thought. We overlook and breeze by them, simply because they don't look like we thought.

> I wonder how many answered prayers, promises, provisions, and God opportunities we miss because they don't look like what we imagine.

I met a young man who told me about his journey to engagement. He said that for the first two years of dating, everything was going fine. Then, during year three, his girlfriend started to question his commitment to the relationship. He reassured her that he was in it for the long haul and eventually they would get engaged. But after five years, she was about to give up and let go, and he sensed it. So he devised a plan one day. He asked her to meet him for dinner at their favorite burger joint. However, on the way to the restaurant he picked up a beautiful two-karat diamond ring from his jeweler. (Apparently he spent all his money on the ring, hence the engagement dinner at the burger joint.) He told her to meet him at their usual spot on the bench right outside the front entrance. He put the diamond ring inside a brown bag from the restaurant, rolled the top down, left it on the bench for her to discover, then went to hide in his car. When she arrived, she saw the "trash" on their bench, threw it away, took a seat, and waited. He was expecting her to discover what was *in* the bag and text him, but she didn't. The longer she waited, the more upset she got, thinking he'd stood her up or was playing a prank. She finally texted him and asked him where he was. He drove up and saw the bag was gone, and she was not happy. He ended up digging through the trash to retrieve the bag and eventually proposed at the restaurant. She did say yes (surprisingly?), but that special moment definitely didn't go how either of them had imagined.

Things in our life often unfold differently than how we imagine. I wonder how many diamonds we miss every day. God is trying to introduce us to something great, but we neglect it, or take it for granted, or are unaware of what's inside because it isn't "wrapped" how we thought. It might be a relationship, a job opportunity, or the answer to your prayer. As with my friend's girlfriend, we need to be careful not to disregard people, moments, and things in our lives. Blessings may not always appear how we expect them to.

In 1 Kings 19, the prophet Elijah's enemies were after him, and he had run into the wilderness. God spoke to him and said, "Go, stand in front of me on the mountain, and I will pass by" (v. 11 NCV). A hurricane wind ripped through the mountains and shattered the rocks, but the Lord wasn't to be found in the wind (the first look). After the wind there was an earthquake, but the Lord wasn't in the earthquake (the second look). After the earthquake came a fire, but the Lord wasn't in the fire (the third look). And after the fire came a gentle, quiet whisper. This was when God spoke to him. This was where God was found…in a whisper.

> God's answers are often in the unassuming… the whispers.

We expect God, expect our solutions, answers, and blessings, to be in the obvious—in the wind, earthquake, and fire. But God's answers are often in the unassuming…the whispers. Too often we're so fixated on how we think God is going to answer our prayer that we overlook it when we receive the answer. It's not wrapped how we thought. What if the person you wrote off is actually the answer to your prayer? What if the open position at work is the next step for you? What if the college that no one is Instagramming about is the right one for you? Look again, and think about it. God often works in mysterious ways.

Greatness Is Often Hidden

In John 9, Jesus encountered a man who was blind from birth. He had compassion for him and wanted to heal him. I'm sure this man had heard about Jesus and worked out in his mind the way his healing would come if he met Jesus. He couldn't see, but he still had an imagination. Would Jesus use a natural remedy? Would He just speak to his ailment or touch his eyes, much like he'd heard about, and instantly he would see perfectly for the first time? The man and those around him were expecting the healing to come the ways they had heard about or seen.

But it was none of the above.

Instead, Jesus bent down, spit on the ground, made some mud, and put it on the man's eyes. Then He commanded him to go to a nearby pool of water and wash his face, and the man went home seeing, completely healed. But no one expected that the way he would recover his eyesight would be through a saliva-and-mud combination. The Pharisees couldn't understand this. Here the Messiah in His greatness was right in front of them, yet they disregarded who He was, and they questioned why He was healing on the Sabbath. Rather than focusing on this man who now had his vision

> Jesus doesn't work in boxes; He has no box.

restored, they focused on why Jesus did the miracle on the day He did it. What? They had formed a box around how God should move, on how and when He answered prayer, and they could not recognize greatness even when it was right in front of them. But Jesus doesn't work in boxes; He has no box.

What if the Pharisees had stopped, stepped out of their box, and looked again? I wonder how much they missed out on, that God wanted to do? I wonder what God has for you that's hidden in obscurity. What if your deliverance or answer to prayer is hidden in the dirt? Oftentimes His greatest work and greatest gifts to us are hidden in the mud of our world. What I've learned is that oftentimes the way God answers our prayers is in unusual forms, often through what many discount. Is your answer in the storm? Disguised by a setback? Could the "package" be in the no? Hidden in what's wrapped in disappointment?

I encourage you to take the time throughout your life to look again, never to be too quick to write off something simply because it doesn't look like you thought it should. Don't write off people who may not appear to be the answer. God will often use the most unsuspecting people to bless, inspire, and encourage you. You never know what God has put inside those who are around you.

Joel Osteen ran Lakewood's television production for seventeen years. He loved working behind the scenes, making sure everything looked as perfect as possible for those who attended the services and for those who watched on television. When his father passed away, there wasn't a pastoral succession plan in place. Joel had never really preached before and had no official training other than what he had learned from his dad. On the outside, he wasn't the ideal pastor. In all those years behind the scenes, I wonder how many realized what was inside him and what God's plan was. Probably not many. It's hard to see the gifts God has put inside people. If you had asked the production crew back in 1999 if they thought Joel could be Lakewood's senior pastor, a *New York Times* best-selling author, and have his own SiriusXM radio channel, they would have said no. They wouldn't have believed it. I imagine they thought Joel would still be doing what he was doing so well back then.

> Jesus was the ultimate gift... wrapped in an unassuming package.

The reality is that we're surrounded by greatness, but it's often hidden. My encouragement is to be a person who isn't quick to write people off or discount them. Take a fresh look at the person next to you at work, in your family, in your dorm. Greatness is often not wrapped up in the way we assume.

Previously, we looked briefly at the family lineage of Jesus, His roots and history, as recorded in Matthew 1. Included in the genealogy is a woman named Rahab, who had been a prostitute and was a Canaanite. David, "the father of Solomon," committed adultery with Bathsheba and plotted the murder of her husband. When Mary, "the mother of Jesus," gave birth to Him, her reputation would have been scandalous. A "virgin birth"? *Sssuuure.* These people were among those who set the stage for Jesus. This was whom He was related to. If God chose Jesus to come from these flawed people, this tells me that greatness can come from the worst environments. Jesus was the ultimate gift...wrapped in an unassuming package.

I'm asking you today to reevaluate your current job and be grateful for it. Ask God to show the reason for which He has you there. It could be a blessing in disguise. Look again at that person before you count them out based on how they look or where they come from. They could be a blessing in disguise. Look again.

Hold On

When you face a major challenge or setback, you may be tempted to give up hope for the future and quit. When you face a closed door, a season-ending injury, or an unexpected setback, it's easy to buy into the "never" lies:

"I'll never get out of debt."

"I'll never reach my dream."

"I'll never get married."

"I'll never be free from this addiction."

Don't believe those never lies that come to all of us when we face disappointment and something seems never to be changing. Hold on to hope and choose to believe that God is going to work everything out for your good. You are a child of God, you have a purpose, and God is going to use *everything*—not just some things, not just the good things—for your good. He's going to work *all* things out for your good, according to Romans 8:28. What a promise!

> God is going to use *everything*—not just some things, not just the good things—for your good.

The flipside of this verse is that the enemy knows you are a person of purpose and destiny, so he's going to try to do everything he can to cause you to lose hope and faith in the promise. He wants you to give up. That is why the writer of Hebrews says, "Let us hold firmly to the faith we profess" (Hebrews 4:14 NIV). It doesn't just say to "hold" but to "hold firmly." Why? Because something is trying to pull your faith away. It's like a tug-of-war. Disappointments come and try to pull it away. You didn't get the promotion, make the team, or get the scholarship, and thoughts come and say, *It's never going to happen.* Time is on the other end pulling against your faith. Thoughts tell you, *It's been too long. You've been waiting forever. Just give up.* Negative voices come and say, *You don't have what it takes. Look what you did. You're a loser.* These are difficult things to navigate through, but this only means one thing: You are worth fighting for! The enemy is aware that you possess purpose and he is attempting to discourage you. The pressures, the setbacks, the depression and anxiety are the challenges. These are all indicators that point us to something that God wants to do in and through us. The enemy is doing everything he can to distract, discourage, and oppose it.

> Fulfilling your destiny and realizing your dreams isn't just about receiving; it's about holding firmly.

He's tempting you to let go of the promise God has for you. And the enemy fights the hardest when he knows God's got something *big* in store for you. So we have to make a decision to hold firmly to our faith in order to become all God has created us to be. Fulfilling your destiny and realizing your dreams isn't just about receiving; it's about holding firmly. In other words, there's a time to ask, to dream, and to receive in our hearts the purpose God has designed for each of our lives. But then there are seasons that require us to hold to it, knowing and trusting that God is going to finish what He started and fulfill His promise.

Here's the great news today: You don't have to hold on by yourself! On your own, it's hard to hold on to hope. When things are pulling you, it gets difficult. But do you know what happens when you stay in faith and hold on to hope? The Bible says that God will "strengthen you with power through his Spirit in your inner being" (Ephesians 3:16 NIV). Your roots will grow and keep you strong. In other words, when you hold on, the Holy Spirit gets involved and helps you, anchors you, strengthens you, and sees you through to the dream. You are provided with His unlimited resources. It's not just on you. You have a Helper. As you hold on to faith, God finishes the work He began in you and every dream will come to pass that He's promised in your life.

Perhaps you're asking: How do I hold on firmly to hope and faith? What does this look like on a daily basis? One key that helps us to hold on to hope is to remember. You have to take time throughout your day, especially in times when you're ready to give up, to remember when God showed up for you in the past.

In our bedroom, we have a large glass vase that's about two feet tall. Within this vase, there are several medium-size rocks. It may appear to be a decorative item to enhance the vibe of our bedroom, but to my family, it's a reminder. Each of those rocks has words and dates we wrote on them that represent a moment when God showed Himself faithful. One rock represents a time when our backs were against the wall financially and God blessed us in a way we didn't see coming. Another rock has "8.11.18" written on it, remembering the day our daughter, Haven, was baptized. If you dig deeper, you will see one that's dated "6.23.22." That was Summer's first flight in seven years. She took a step of faith, despite her vertigo, and God met her and sustained her through the whole trip with no issues! I could go on and on. These are milestones for our family. Times when we didn't know how God was going to turn things around, when we faced a setback, and God did a miracle. Those rocks remind our family of times when God provided for us, when He changed our lives. Every day when we walk by the vase, we're reminded that He's done the impossible before, and He can do it again.

It's so easy to forget what God has done for us and what He's given us. Most of us are surrounded by miracles and God's provision, but we lose sight of them. While you are holding on for your next miracle, it's good to remember the miracles God has done. It's remembering that fuels your faith and hope as you walk through your present challenges. Whether it's filling a jar with rocks or keeping a journal, being intentional about remembering typically leads to being grateful for what God has done in your life and where He's taken you from and to. Gratitude is a powerful force that stirs up hope in us.

Take Inventory

There was a widow in 2 Kings 4 who had lost her husband and was in serious financial trouble. When she cried out to the prophet Elisha for help, he asked her what she had in her house. She told him that they had nothing at all, except a small jar of oil. Notice that the prophet didn't focus her attention on how much she lacked or how much money she needed to pay the debt. He shifted her perspective from what she had lost to what she had left. He told her to gather all the empty jars she could find, begin pouring the oil she had left into them, and God supernaturally extended the oil to fill every jar. She sold the oil, paid her debts, and she and her sons lived on what was left.

> While you are holding on for your next miracle, it's good to remember the miracles God has done.

The point is that what the widow had left in her house was more than enough for God to do a miracle. God doesn't need a lot to do a lot. Whatever you have is all that God needs. Stop looking at what you lost, at what didn't work out, and know that you have all you need for God to do a miracle. Throughout the Scripture, Jesus seemed to always redirect people to what they had left. When He fed the five thousand in Matthew 14, He asked the disciples what food they had left. He didn't ask them how many pizzas He needed to buy for the masses. He focused the disciples on what was in their hands. They handed Him the boy's lunch of five loaves and two fish, and Jesus blessed it and multiplied it. Whatever you have left in your life is enough for Jesus to bless and multiply. Change your perspective from what you don't have to what you have left. Choose to be grateful for what you have, and He will bless and multiply it.

> Change your perspective from what you don't have to what you have left.

Shortly after I started dating Summer, she invited me to "officially" meet her parents. God has taught me a lot through them, starting with the very first time I hung out with them as a family. They invited me for a day out on the river on their boat, and let's just say I was a *little* nervous. Summer gave me the directions to the boat launch, and as I approached the park, I turned onto the street they had told me. Seconds after I turned, I was shocked to see red-and-blue flashing lights in my rearview mirror. My mind raced through all the reasons why I was getting pulled over, but nothing made sense. I wasn't speeding, and my blinker was on. The police officer walked up to my car and told me that I had made a left-hand turn on a street that didn't allow left-hand turns. Apparently I had missed the sign. He asked for my license and registration, which I handed over, and he walked back to the patrol car. Moments later, my phone rang. It was Summer. My heart was pounding. What was I going to tell her? I had left early to make sure that I would arrive on time to make a good impression, but now I was late. What was her dad thinking?

I was about to answer the phone when the officer returned to my car. As he handed me my license and registration back, he told me that my license had expired. I had just accepted a job in Houston, and in the weeks leading up to the move, I had decided that it didn't make sense to pay for a license renewal in a state I was leaving in a month. Well, now it made sense. He asked me to step out of the car and told me that I couldn't drive my car on an expired license. I tried to explain my situation, but it didn't matter. He had already called a tow truck. My phone rang again, and Summer asked where I was. I explained the situation, and I could hear her dad in the background say he was going to walk to where I was since it was only minutes away. So there I was, standing by a tow truck and a cop as my new girlfriend's dad approached to "officially" meet me. I was thinking, *Hey, Mr. Schiavo, I know this looks really bad, but I promise I'm responsible. I promise I can take good care of your daughter. I know what this looks like, but this in no way is a reflection of my character.*

Despite what most dads would have probably done in that moment, Kevin greeted me with a smile and a tight handshake and then proceeded to try to convince the cop to give me some grace. I couldn't believe it! I was in the wrong, yet Kevin was defending me. It was awesome. Unfortunately, the cop didn't budge, so we both stood as we watched my car getting towed away. The awkward silence lasted for about thirty seconds, and then he looked at me and said, "Let's go tubing!" We had the best time that day; however, it felt as though he accelerated a little aggressively when he pulled me on the tube, perhaps a subtle reminder that I was dating *his* daughter. I learned a few things that day—in addition to the fact that Sum's dad is a man of grace, generosity, and has a great sense of humor. What's interesting is that once we got in the boat and started to get to know one another and make memories, I *quickly* forgot about my car, which was somewhere in a local auto impound. I unintentionally forgot about what I had lost, because I was fully enjoying what I had…an amazing girl and "dream" future in-laws.

Fast-forward to my first Thanksgiving dinner with Sum and her parents. I was a little nervous about our first formal dinner together as we sat down at the table. After we settled in, her mom, Debby, lit a candle and said she wanted us to go around the table and share some things we were thankful for. My stomach dropped. I wasn't used to doing anything

> You don't have to light a candle today, but maybe it's time for you to pause and think about the things you have.

like this in a family setting. This required intentional thought, and then actually verbalizing those thoughts in front of everyone. Debby started and immediately set the tone. Though I found it uncomfortable at first, as I heard everyone's perspective on their life, reflecting and appreciating what they had and who they had in their life, it changed me. By the end, I was crying like a baby and it turned out to be one of the best Thanksgivings ever. It changed my perspective on what I already had. I was "forced" to take inventory of my life and identify what I was grateful for. You don't have to light a candle today, but maybe it's time for you to pause and think about the things you have. Think about people and things for which you are grateful. Why not pause and write on a sheet of paper some things you are grateful for in your life right now?

Don't Take for Granted What Is Another Person's Miracle

My wife inspires me every day. Summer reminds me daily of the power of perspective. If you know Summer, you would probably describe her as someone who is full of life, joy, and passion...all on display in her captivating smile, which stole my heart. There is pure joy found in her smile. Not only is it beautiful and complements her gorgeous brown eyes, but her smile radiates life and possibility. We've been married for more than nineteen years, and her smile still gets me. But it moves me now on a much deeper level than it did in the years after we first met, when that smile came so naturally. Now I know there are days when that smile is a choice. In chapter 3, I wrote that after a flight several years ago, Summer's world began to spin...quite literally. We don't know what happened, but since that flight, she has battled vertigo every day. We've seen specialists, ENTs, some of the best doctors in Houston, and we have no solutions. The dizziness is constant, with driving, riding elevators, and other types of motion making it worse. It limits her physically in so many ways. She battles mind games every day, with lies from the enemy saying, "You'll never be healed. You'll never get your normal life back."

Summer has prayed, we have prayed, others have prayed and are praying, but she hasn't been healed yet. Early on, we asked why a lot. We've seen other people get healed speedily. We've seen God do the impossible in our lives. Why is this not changing? Over time, Summer has made the very difficult choice to move from why to what. I've heard her pray prayers such as, "God, I don't understand this, but I trust You. I'm choosing to believe that healing is coming and You are somehow working this for my good. I'm holding on. I'm staying in faith!" In other moments,

I've heard her pray, "God, I know that You don't waste our pain. I believe You are building a well within me that I and others will be able to draw from in my future. I'm believing for a well of character, understanding, and empathy."

If you didn't know Summer, and you met her today, you would never know what she was battling because she chooses to smile

> "What one may see as ordinary, another sees as a miracle."

despite how she feels. She worships. She gives. She fights to hold on to the hope in the promise that God not only heals, but works all things out for her good. Despite the fact that she can't do a lot of things she wishes she could do, she chooses to believe that there is redemptive purpose in her pain. Sum often tells others who ask about how she's feeling that "it could always be worse." She consistently takes time to be thankful for what she can do. She's quick to remind me that for some people it's a miracle to be able to talk or to walk or to have children. In other words, she chooses not to focus on what she doesn't get to do, but what she can do.

Craig Johnson is a friend and pastor at Lakewood who often says, "What one may see as ordinary, another sees as a miracle." He and his wife, Sam, have a son named Connor who has autism. The Johnsons are legends in my book. They fight to choose to be grateful, not for what they don't have, but for what they do have. Their faith journey has evolved into Craig starting Champions Club, a global ministry serving kids, teens, and adults with special needs and the medically fragile. These clubs help and give hope to individuals with autism, Down syndrome, cerebral palsy, and other diagnoses and medical conditions. Much like Summer, Craig and Sam could choose to be victims, to complain and focus on what isn't right or working, but instead they have chosen to trust God, to trust His promise, to choose to be grateful for what they have, and to serve others facing similar challenges.

My friend Justin "JP" Lane joined the army in 2008 at the age of twenty. As he watched the Twin Towers fall in 2001, JP knew he wanted to join the military when he was old enough. As a combat engineer, he was deployed to Afghanistan as a specialist with the 428th Engineer Company in October 2010 to search for IEDs (improvised explosive devices). In July 2011, his RG-31 truck was penetrated by a 200-pound IED while on a mission. He was in a coma for six weeks and had twenty-eight surgeries, which changed his life forever. JP is a double amputee, and the doctors told him he wasn't going to be able to do many things, such as use prosthetics because his legs were so badly damaged or speak properly again because of a tracheotomy. He has proven them wrong. JP will tell you he joined the army to serve and protect the American people, and by the grace of God, he still does. He is an inspirational speaker who promotes post-traumatic growth to combat-wounded veterans and others across the country, helping them build a mind-set to "never give up and never surrender." His journey of faith, determination, and love of life is inspiring. What stands out to me every time I'm around JP is how thankful he is. He's thankful to walk, to breathe, and to laugh. JP told his story at Lakewood, and I was reminded once again of the things I take for granted that others consider a miracle. Hearing his story puts my issues and what I could complain about in perspective.

Today, maybe you are in a very difficult season and holding on by a thread. You may feel like nothing is going to change. Let me encourage you to: "Take a new grip with your tired hands" (Hebrews 12:12 NLT). It's time to take a new grip on your promise and your purpose. I believe this begins with remembering that

God has never failed you before and He won't start now. It begins with shifting your focus from what you lost to what you have left.

Hold on...*doors* are going to open.

Hold on...*victory* is coming.

Hold on...*healing* is coming.

I believe and declare that as you hold on, dreams you thought were dead are being resurrected and you will experience a new inner strength. You will be able to say, "Despite what it looks like, I'm holding on to hope, and I'm livin' the dream!"

CHAPTER TWELVE

POWER MOVES

Find Significance in Serving Others

I n today's culture, the word *influencer* is commonly understood to refer solely to those who have YouTube channels and blue checks by their names. But that's the farthest thing from the truth. Whether you realize it or not, if you are breathing right now, you have been given a measure of influence. You possess the ability to affect the hearts, behaviors, and development of other people.

In 2017, I was on a ministry trip in Switzerland for ten days while Summer stayed home with the kids. Denver was seven at the time, and to help him better understand where I was, Summer bought a small globe and sat down with him. She showed him where Houston was, then took his finger and dragged it across the globe to where I was in Switzerland. He was fascinated, so Summer spent time slowly spinning the globe and showing him many of the famous places in the world. After a few minutes, Summer leaned over him and whispered into his ear, "Denver, you are going to change the world."

> What are you going to change the world into?

Denver slowly spun the globe, obviously thinking intently, then innocently asked, "Change it into *what*?"

He was profoundly right. The question isn't whether you *will* change the world. We've all been given a measure of influence to impact the world around us. The right question is: What are you going to change the world into?

I hope you believe that you are a person who is changing the world. Just by your presence, you impact every person you meet and every space into which you walk. What's important is to know the most effective way you can positively impact and change the world around you, and fortunately for us, Jesus tells us how.

Power, Influence, and Position

In the Scripture, the mother of two of Jesus' disciples, James and John, came to Jesus with a request: "In your Kingdom, please let my two sons sit in places of honor next to you, one on your right and the other on your left" (Matthew 20:21 NLT). She was just being a mom who wanted the best for her boys and wasn't meaning to stir up trouble, but the other ten disciples heard it and were outraged. Although she looked like she was the problem here, the real problem was that she asked publicly for what all the disciples *secretly* wanted in their hearts—power, influence, and position.

Jesus called them together and said, "You know that the rul-
ers in this world *lord* it over their people, and officials flaunt their
authority over those under them. But among you it will be *different.* Whoever wants to be a leader among you must be your
servant, and whoever wants to be
first among you must become your
slave. For even the Son of Man
came not to be served but to *serve
others* and to give his life as a ran-
som for many" (vv. 25–28 NLT).
Imagine the reaction of the
mom and the disciples who heard this. It was just as counter culture then as it is now. Today's culture is obsessed with fame, status, and position as never before. Jesus says to us, "But with you,
it has to be different." Instead of pursuing fame, Jesus invites us
to pursue greatness. There is a big difference, and we all know it.
We all know famous people who are not great people, and there
are great people you work with or live by who aren't famous.

> Instead of pursuing
> fame, Jesus invites us
> to pursue greatness.

Instead of pursuing fame, Jesus invites us to pursue greatness.
He's saying, "I'm empowering you, giving you keys to the Kingdom, not for attention, but for authority." It's an authority that is
demonstrated in Exodus 17. Joshua was leading the Israelite military into battle while Moses, Aaron, and Hur stood on the hill.
As long as Moses held up his staff, God caused the Israelites to
advance. But when Moses got too weak to hold his arms up, Aaron
and Hur found a stone for him to sit on. Then they stood on each
side of Moses and held up his hands until sunset. As a result,
Joshua and the Israelites won the battle. It appears that Joshua and
Moses were the heroes and received all the attention, but this win
came only because two men without titles and status were willing
to serve. Who were the real heroes, the most powerful persons

here? There's no doubt that Aaron and Hur provided the power source. They exercised their authority by lifting someone else's arms. Exodus 17:13 states that the victory came "as a result" of Aaron and Hur.

This story challenges our perspective of power.

I believe I'm writing to Aarons and Hurs today, to leaders and influencers. When you walk into your workplace, your relationships, or your social circles, you may not be in the spotlight, but you're choosing to lift others, to put stones in place, to lift arms, and as a result, others are winning. What's happening? You are exercising true authority and power. You're not worried about position, status, or fame. Your focus is on being great.

> Who's winning as a result of you holding up their arms?

Do you see that attention is about us, and authority is about others? Regardless of our position, whether you're a student or professor, accountant or CEO, stay-at-home mom or lawyer, any measure of influence we are given from God is given for the benefit of others. Your dream, purpose, gifts, talents, and platform are not just for you; they are for others. How are you exercising your power? Who's winning as a result of you holding up their arms?

Significance, Fulfilment, and Satisfaction

I have a friend named Chad who took a step of faith out of his corporate job to live the dream he felt God put in his heart. He began to buy and flip properties in Houston one at a time, and in just four years he flipped over one hundred properties all over Texas and had to hire an entire team of employees. He's a go-getter, and after the hundredth property was purchased, I asked him, "When will you be content? When's enough? What motivates you to keep growing and expanding?" Chad told me that he'd watched a documentary about a famous billionaire who gave away more money in one year than a significant number of churches and charities combined. He said it disturbed him, and he determined to help change that statistic. He said that his dream is to

> Leadership, influence, and power are about serving and helping others.

live on 10 percent of his income and give 90 percent of it to the church and charities, helping others and advancing good causes.

As a result of Chad living his dream, many others are going higher. Whether it's his employees, or flood victims receiving his donations, or under-resourced schools getting necessary funds, his influence is helping others. In fact, I wrote most of this book in rental homes Chad invited me to use for free. It's easy to be generous when you have a hundred properties, but Chad was just as generous when he only had one. Chad is a powerful man who exercises great authority because he lives to give and to help others, and God continues to expand his world.

Leadership, influence, and power are about serving and helping others. This is where you discover great significance, fulfillment, and satisfaction.

I read about a football coach who took over a Division 1 college program that had performed poorly for years. Despite this, Devonte, a high school standout, was interested in playing at the college, even though he was heavily recruited by far better schools. The coach met with the young superstar and tried to sign him, but Devonte would only give a verbal commitment, stating that he wanted to wait to sign until after the football season ended. The coach was desperate to get him and told him he would hold a scholarship for him. Through the fall and winter, other college recruiters kept showing up and trying to get this amazing talent to change his mind and come to their school. In the spring, the coach met with Devonte, asking him to finally officially sign with the college, which he did. When he asked the seventeen-year-old star why he waited so long, the coach was astonished to hear Devonte explain that it was because most of his teammates weren't being recruited earlier in the year. He hoped that by not signing anywhere, all the college coaches who kept coming to see him play would discover how good some of his teammates were and recruit them. At an age when most people are self-centered, this young man was already thinking of his impact on others, using his influence and position to serve others. He could have easily just made sure he took care of himself and gotten signed on day one. That wouldn't have been wrong, but he exercised his power through serving, and as a result, many of his teammates received scholarships.

The Power of the Towel

As with Chad and Devonte, God intends that you use your gifts, platform, promotion, and influence to benefit others. Jesus said that the difference He expected to see in His disciples was how they stewarded their influence, and then He demonstrated what He meant. On the final night before His death, He wanted to leave a lasting impression in His disciples' minds of true authority and ultimate power. They had seen Him walk on water, resurrect a boy at a funeral, and multiply a Happy Meal to feed thousands. They had seen His power displayed countless times, but He saved His best power move for last.

In John 13, after a long day of walking and ministering, Jesus and His disciples entered a room to share the Passover meal but there was no servant to wash their feet as was the custom of the day. Roads were full of animal droppings, so feet needed to be cleaned upon arrival. All the disciples found seats, assuming someone else in the room would take that job. There must have been an awkward pause, and then the Scripture says that Jesus, "knowing that the Father had given Him all *authority*," got up and assumed the most powerful position He could take with His influence. Jesus, the King of kings and Lord of lords, who holds the universe

> Jesus, the King of kings and Lord of lords, who holds the universe in His hands, removed His robe, took a towel, and washed their dirty feet.

in His hands, removed His robe, took a towel, and washed their dirty feet. He did not bypass any of them because of their past lack of faith or questionings or even the failures that would follow in the days ahead. Ten would desert Him, one would deny Him, and one would betray Him. He knew what they would do. Yet he got down on the ground and washed the animal droppings off their feet. Even Judas's.

The disciples were stunned. Speechless. They saw most of his power moves, but could this move of washing dirty feet be the most powerful? The one that left the greatest impression? Absolutely.

Jesus then said, "Since I, your Lord and teacher, have washed your feet, you ought to wash each other's feet. I have given you an example to follow." In other words, the towel showed them what *real* power looked like. Of all the things He could have done in the moments before His betrayal and trial, He didn't teach them about preaching eloquently, or how to grow a church in five ways, or give them a three-point lesson on strategic leadership. He grabbed a towel and showed them how to exercise authority. He was saying, "Live and lead from this position and place. Move in your world from this position of love." It's not about titles or status; it's about your towel. That's where the real power is.

It's time to show our world what power looks like. And it's not just serving and lifting those we love, but serving all types of people. It's not just your circle, but all circles. The Passover supper has ended, our feet are wet with His grace, and He's given us the example. It's time to make a difference. You have been given influence to serve people. Your "new levels" are there. Get your towel and exercise this position of power and watch God fill you with deep significance and satisfaction. Like Chad and Devonte, serve others and watch God take you places you haven't even dreamed!

Can I Get a Witness?

In Acts 22, the apostle Paul, who at one time persecuted the early church, describes how Jesus had transformed his life and called him to be a witness of Jesus. God spoke to Paul through a man named Ananias in Damascus, who said, "The God of our ancestors has chosen you to know Him, to be His witness, and to tell everyone what you have seen and heard." It's interesting that the word *witness* in the original text is the same word we use for a witness in a common trial. In a court case, the role of the witness is simply to testify—to describe what they have seen, heard, felt, and experienced. "I was there, and this is what happened. These are the facts that I know."

> This is His plan for you and me—to reveal Himself to others through us.

This became Paul's purpose. He derived his income as a tent-maker, which was his nine-to-five, but he realized he was not *just* building tents. He discovered that he had been designed to honor God *through* his tentmaking and his lifestyle. He was called to build lives, to help build the Kingdom. God wanted to make His appeal to the Gentiles through Paul as a witness, to reveal Himself through Paul. And this is His plan for you and me—to reveal Himself to others through us.

I recently went to the funeral for the father of one of our Lakewood staff members. My friend Tara spoke powerfully about how her father's legacy was living on through the family. His smile could be seen in his daughter's smile, his work ethic could be seen in his other child, and his creativity was carried on in another. Yes, he went on to Heaven, but you could still see him in his kids, in those he loved and lived with, in those who shared his DNA. Tara was saying, "If you didn't know my dad, and you want to, just spend some time with us kids and you will see him." This really spoke to me. In the same way, we are God's kids, and there are unique attributes of God in each of us. He shaped us, breathed life into us, and we uniquely reflect our Creator. He can be seen through us. We are living witnesses to what God is like.

But if you are like me, sometimes my role as a witness seems to expand to a different seat in the "courtroom of life," so to speak. It's easy to move into the judge's seat. After you've been on your faith journey for some time, your experiences with God may seem to diminish and you begin to grow a bit numb and callous. If you start to lose sight of your own need for grace, the judge's seat gets more comfortable. It's easy to get critical and judgmental of others and lose sight of being a witness of God's grace. But God is the only One worthy to judge anyone, not me or you. I've learned that I will always need God's grace in my life, and my role is always to give grace to others as well as the benefit of the doubt, not to judge them.

Another seat that can be tempting to take is the prosecutor's seat. The prosecutor's role is to press charges and accuse people. That is not our role as believers. It's the role of the enemy. The Bible describes him as the "accuser of the brethren," who says things such as "not good enough, not doing enough, look at all the mistakes you've made, you can't serve God." His job is to condemn, to accuse, to discourage, to attack people's minds and convince them to believe lies about themselves and their destiny. He doesn't need our help. Stay far away from that seat.

Lastly, there's the defense chair. Oh, it's easy to get comfortable in this role and pretend to serve as a defense attorney for God. But God doesn't need a defense. He doesn't need you to argue for Him. Look at the mountains, the oceans, the stars, the galaxies, the universe. God is big enough to handle things. If you think God *needs* a defense, your God is too small.

God has simply called us to live as witnesses. Most of the time, people are not convinced by facts. They are convinced by others' experiences, by the evidence of the fruit of one's life. Being a witness means bringing out and displaying the qualities and characteristics of God in how you live, how you love, and how you work. It's not a role reserved for pastors, teachers, missionaries, or others who are in "the ministry." Yes, those are significant roles and positions, but the reality is that every believer is a minister. Whatever your career path is, whatever your passion is, whatever your social network is, that's *your* ministry. It's just as impactful and significant because it's yours, and you are reflecting a part of God that He's made you to be. You are a witness in the place God has you in right now.

I loved show-and-tell when I was in elementary school. At the beginning of the week, we would bring something unique and valuable to us, perhaps a toy, and put it on display in the classroom. All throughout the week the students observed what was brought, took notes, and prepared questions. Then on Friday, each student had an opportunity to stand up in front of the class with their object and tell about it. That was a simple, yet profound concept.

> Being a witness means bringing out and displaying the qualities and characteristics of God in how you live, how you love, and how you work.

In 1 Peter 3, it says to keep your hearts at attention before Christ, to be ready to speak up and tell anyone who asks *why* you're living the way you are, and to always do it with the utmost courtesy. Peter's assumption is that the believers are living, working, loving, walking through difficulties, handling their money, and leading their families in such a way that people are asking them why they live the way they do. In other words, Peter is saying, "When the opportunities present themselves, show and tell."

I've heard it said, "Preach the gospel at all times, and if necessary use words." I know the importance of preaching the gospel with words, but the point is that you don't have to be the loudest to make the biggest impact. Often the most influential people speak softly but live loudly—with character, with generosity, with compassion and excellence. May your life be lived in such a way that people ask questions. May your work be of such excellence that people ask what motivates you. It doesn't matter where we work, how old we are, or where we've been, each of us carries purpose. Each of us has been called to be a witness right where we are. To be a witness means you're not sitting back and being influenced by your circumstances and surroundings, by what's

> God's appeal
> to your world is
> through you!

trending and popular, but you're stepping into every space with a mission to shine, to lift, to encourage, to show Jesus to people.

You may not like your current job, but keep in mind that someone there needs what you have. You may not like your apartment, but what if a neighbor needs what you have? Wherever God has placed you, there is great purpose. God's appeal to your world is through you. Wherever you go, make it your focus to be a person who lifts others, whose presence changes boardrooms, neighborhoods, and locker rooms.

The One

The question of how we can influence the world can feel overwhelming, but what if changing your world didn't start with the concept of impacting millions or even hundreds? What if changing the world began with *one*? Luke 10:27 states that the most important commandments are to love God and love your neighbor. He simplified the way to bring change to our world to *one* person. Don't get overwhelmed by the idea of changing the masses and overlook the one—that person working next to you, your teammate, or the person across the street.

It's amazing what can happen when you impact one person. There was a young man named Sam Martin who lived in a small East Texas town in 1939. Sam was so passionate about his faith that every morning he would go to the high school and write Scriptures on the chalkboard. One night one of his seventeen-year-old classmates was walking home from a nightclub at two in the morning and began to think about Heaven and where he would spend eternity. When he got home, he randomly opened the big family Bible to a painting of Jesus standing at a door and knocking, with a Bible verse that read: "If anyone will open the door, I will come in." This young man's heart was stirred, and he remembered that was the same Scripture that Sam had written on the chalkboard at school. He called Sam early that morning and asked, "Why do you think I am feeling this way?" Sam replied, "That

> What if changing your world didn't start with the concept of impacting millions or even hundreds? What if changing the world began with *one*?

is God drawing you." That Sunday morning Sam took his new friend to church. That was the day that John Osteen, Joel's father, made a decision to follow Christ. You've probably never heard of Sam Martin, but you've probably heard of John Osteen. Over eighty years ago, one person impacted one person, who would go on to found Lakewood Church and impact millions for Christ all over the world and still is. Little did Sam Martin know that this one invitation would lead to the largest church in America's history.

What if Sam had thought, *Why write these Bible verses on the chalkboard? No one cares, and I'm sick of getting made fun of for doing it. Why stand out? Why go against the grain?* I'm grateful that he didn't let those thoughts stop him. It's never I "just" brought one, invited one, impacted one. You never know the impact of the one, for in the one *is* the power to change the world.

Rather than changing the whole team, maybe it's changing and investing into one teammate. Rather than the whole neighborhood, maybe it's your next-door neighbor. Rather than your whole family, maybe it's your brother or sister.

Changing your world starts with impacting one person.

Just Show Up

The apostle Paul paints an interesting picture of the conditions he probably often experienced during his missionary journeys: "When we arrived in Macedonia, there was no rest for us. We faced conflict from every direction, with battles on the outside and fear on the inside. But God, who encourages those who are discouraged, encouraged us by the arrival of Titus. *His presence was a joy*, but so was the news he brought" (2 Corinthians 7:5–7 NLT).

Struggles, conflicts, no rest, and fears. Sounds a lot like the environments we engage in every day in our world, and perhaps at work and in our family. But look what happened when one man, Titus, came into it. His presence brought joy and a lift, and so did his words. One man influenced an anxiety-filled space. One man showed up and impacted people. He brought joy and life and changed the culture of that space in Macedonia. The light of God's presence inside him permeated the struggle and the anxiety. Even though he was tired from his travels and had things he was dealing with, he didn't allow the culture there and what was happening to get inside and disrupt and discourage him. He understood his purpose and possessed the power in Christ to be able to come into the mess without the mess getting in him. Titus's impact began simply in the fact that he showed up. Your presence is the source of ministry, influence, and impact.

When I was growing up, my dad worked through a lot of

challenges, but one thing he did was *show up*. He was there for my games, teacher conferences, and activities. He wasn't perfect, but he was *present*. It wasn't so much about what he said; it was about the power of his presence. He modeled so many important things to me, tried his best to introduce us kids to faith, and gave it his best shot, given the cards that he was dealt. He showed me he cared and gave me the most valuable thing he had—his time.

> Dads show up. Spouses show up. Friends show up. Never underestimate the power of showing up.

Dads show up. Spouses show up. Friends show up. Never underestimate the power of showing up.

I have two friends whom I've known for twenty-plus years: Chad Bruegman and Sonny Savitski. They are on my dream team. I mentioned them previously in the book. Beyond being men of character and phenomenal leaders in their own spaces, they are the people in my life who simply "show up." They've been there to celebrate my successes and good times with me. In times when I've been discouraged, when I've gotten the worst news, when a family member passed away, they showed up. They don't always have answers, but their presence speaks. One thing stands out: They simply are friends who have shown up for me and influenced my life and so many others.

I'm sure that the people who have had the most impact on you are the ones who have shown up, especially in life's critical moments. It's not so much what they say as that they show up and impact with the ministry of their presence...in hospital rooms, at games, at funerals, and graduations. Let's be people who form the habit of showing up for people in our lives.

Enlarging Your World

You may be familiar with the family board game called Life. You draw a career or a paycheck, then you spin to see how many kids you get. You focus on accumulating money and as many houses and other assets to beat the other players. The goal of the game isn't to give or share; the goal is to possess as much stuff as possible. At the end of the game, when the winner has all the stuff and has posted his celebration on Instagram, *it all goes back in the box.*

If we're not careful, we can embrace this board game approach to our own real lives. We can make accumulating stuff and money our *top* priority, but in the end it all just goes back in the box. I'm not saying we shouldn't work hard, save, and invest wisely for a great future. But one of the keys to the abundant life that Jesus invites us into is to choose to live generously. Throughout Scripture, we discover Jesus teaching ways to live that are counter culture and don't come naturally to most of us. "Love and pray for your enemies." "Rejoice when you face trials." "Rush to the back of the line and wait to be called forward." "It is better to give than to receive." It doesn't say that receiving isn't good; it says giving is *better.* It's better because of what it does for others and for what it does in us.

> One of the best ways you can show God to people is by giving.

My daughter, Haven, and I had stopped at a gas station one evening. As I was putting gas into my car, I noticed a distraught-looking man who was standing motionless by his car at the pump next to us. I asked him if he was okay, and he shook his head no. He told me he was on his way to visit his family in Louisiana, but he was out of gas and money. So I handed him the cash I had in my wallet, looked him in the eyes, and said, "God bless you, man." He paused and just stared at me, then he said, "He just did." That was true, whether it's money or time or your talents, when you give, you are putting the love of God on display for others to experience. One of the best ways you can show God to people is by giving. It might just be a smile or a compliment, or a few bucks at a gas station. The result? People experience the love of God through you, and your world, inside and out, begins to expand.

In 2008, I took a team of ten young adults to Africa for two weeks to partner with an organization there that brings hope and help to the needy. When we arrived at the airport in Botswana, the luggage of four of the girls had been lost in transit. Can you imagine them spending the first four days in a Third World country for the first time with no extra clothes or shoes, no blow dryers, makeup, personal items... nothing. The girls who had their luggage did their best to share, but let's just say that those first days were rough.

But something began to shift in our team after our first day of serving people in a village. As we were helping two different families rebuild the straw roofs on their huts, we experienced what their daily lives were like. We could hear kids laughing while kicking a soccer ball around. We saw smiling women as they walked together to draw water. There were no phones, air conditioners, or any of the conveniences we enjoy every day, yet they seemed to be happy and content. When our team returned to where we were staying that evening, no one complained about not having a hair dryer or a clean T-shirt. We laughed, ate, and reflected on how the villagers had taught us a lesson in life. You can have what appears to be next to nothing and still be happy. Happiness is found inside. When the luggage arrived days later, can you guess what the girls did? They took their clothes and shoes and things they "needed" so badly, and they gave them all away. It was a life-changing moment they will never forget.

You don't have to live long or acquire much to quickly realize that more money and stuff can never satisfy you. We were made for something this world can't offer, and we won't find it if we play life's game in a way our Creator didn't design it to be played. What would happen if you started to make giving more of a priority than getting? You would experience what Haven and I did that night at the gas station—the feeling and realization that God was using you to make Himself known to someone in need. You would begin to experience the abundance He promised that comes in the form of peace and joy when you give your time and talents to someone else or a cause bigger than your own.

> What would happen if you started to make giving more of a priority than getting?

Remember that Jesus didn't come to make bad people good. He came to make dead people alive! Alive to generosity, alive to peace, love, grace, and purity. Our mission is less about being the guardians of morality and more about being guides to the Master.

Proverbs 11:24 says, "The world of the generous gets larger and larger; the world of the stingy gets smaller and smaller" (MSG). Life, true life, the abundant life Jesus promised, isn't found in getting; it's discovered and won by giving. Let's start winning today. You have one life, so spend it wisely on things

> Life, true life, the abundant life Jesus promised, isn't found in getting; it's discovered and won by giving.

that matter, on serving and giving your time to help others, on sowing into the Kingdom. You will discover the abundant life that God promises…right here, right now…in the space of giving. In fact, I'm believing and declaring that as you live generously, your world is expanding, and your heart is expanding. New opportunities are coming your way, and not only will you be someone's miracle, but God will send you miracles.

God is about to enlarge your world in such a way that you will be able to say, "I'm givin' and I'm livin' the dream!"

CHAPTER THIRTEEN

THE DREAM AWAITS

There's More for You

When my daughter, Haven, was little, she was afraid to ride her first bike without training wheels. Like any good parent, I pulled out my bribing skills. I promised her that if she rode her bike without the training wheels, I would take her to Target to pick out *anything* she wanted. I went all in. Yes, I was desperate. At that point, I thought she was done trying for the day and wouldn't take me up on the offer. But I was wrong. She heard the word *Target* and immediately grabbed her helmet! I helped her on the bike to make one last attempt for the day, and it was as though she knew how to ride the whole time. She took off all by herself, with no help needed. She not only cruised down the sidewalk, but managed to turn in the neighbor's driveway and ride all the way back to me. Looking back now, I have a feeling I got hustled. She got off her bike, looked me squarely in the eyes, and said, "Let's go to Target!"

As we walked into Target, I had no idea what this determined little girl had on her mind. As we walked by the big-screen televisions, she didn't slow down. I breathed a sigh of relief. Then she passed the life-size Barbie dolls and didn't waver. Another sigh of relief. The game stations? No. Haven has always been a strong-minded, resolute girl, and she knew what she wanted. Turning into a toy aisle, she walked to the end, bent down, and grabbed a five-dollar Polly Pocket doll, held it up to me, and said, "This one, Dad. I want this."

> Could you be limiting God by your requests? By your thinking? By your expectations?

I was shocked by her choice. I asked, "Are you sure?" I had promised her whatever she picked out and was prepared for the worst. I was ready to have a difficult conversation with Summer about the unreasonable purchase and why I did it. But Haven insisted on the Polly Pocket, so we walked out together with my bank account still intact. I would have purchased her something so much more expensive, yet all she wanted was that doll.

Now I know she was a kid and had a limited perspective, but it caused me to think about my life. I asked myself, "Have I set my sights and expectations too low when God has the capability to do so much more in my life? How many times do I settle for something that's less than God's best?" How about you? Could you be limiting God by your requests? By your thinking? By your expectations? Do you have an "I'm not good enough" mentality that says you don't deserve anything better than what you've experienced? Are you keeping your hopes and expectations low so you won't be let down or disappointed? God wants to be good to you. He wants to move in your life. Your best days are not behind you; they are still in front of you. It is often our own expectations and thoughts that limit what God wants to do in our lives.

Good Enough Is Not Good Enough

In Mark 8, some people brought a blind man to Jesus, hoping He would heal him. Jesus took the blind man by the hand and led him out of the town. Then He spit on the man's eyes, put his hands on him, and asked him, "Can you see anything?" The man looked around and replied, "Yes, I see people, but they look like trees walking around." Then Jesus placed His hands on the man's eyes again, and his eyes were restored and saw clearly.

It's hard not to be distracted by the means that Jesus used in this man's healing—spit. It leads me to believe that God will often use unusual, sometimes unorthodox ways to get you what you need. Regardless of how Jesus healed in that moment, what's clear was His desire to see this man fully healed. His desire for you isn't that you become half of what you were designed to be. His plan is that you become *all* you were designed to be. After the first touch, this man could see. That was a miracle, and it was better than what he had experienced. He may have thought, *This is good enough.* But Jesus didn't want to just usher in some improvement. He wanted to do more in his life. He wanted to completely restore his sight.

Many people settle for what they think is good enough. Good enough may be okay, and we should be grateful for it, but the Bible says God will lead us on the *best* pathway for our lives. His plan is to fully finish the work He starts in your life, not partially finish it. He wants to fully change and transform you into the person He's designed you to be. He wants you to live the life of purpose and destiny He's called you to fulfill. Don't be okay with mediocrity or just getting by. It's time to be fully free and walk in the fullness of all He has planned for you!

God led the Israelites out of Egyptian captivity and into freedom with a promise to bring them into a land flowing with milk and honey. It was the promise of a prosperous future. However, when they got halfway there, the Israelites wanted to stop and turn back. They wanted to make permanent what God had designed to be temporary. The food that God provided for them every day in the wilderness was manna. It was good, and it sustained them, but God had milk and honey in store for them. What happened? They talked themselves into permanently settling in a place or returning to a place from which God had delivered them. What am I saying? Look back and be grateful for where God has brought you, but keep believing and expecting God's best for your life. Don't put a stake down and settle for good when God has His best in front of you. You've had good opportunities, relationships, and victories. Be grateful for them, but stir your faith and continue to look forward to the promises that are in front of you.

> Don't put a stake down and settle for good when God has His best in front of you.

Don't Settle

In John 19, when the soldiers had crucified Jesus, "They put his garments into four piles, one for each of them. But they said,

'Let's not tear up his robe,' for it was seamless. 'Let's throw dice
to see who gets it.' This fulfilled the Scripture that says, 'They
divided my clothes among them and cast lots for my robe"' (vv.
22–24 TLB). Then they kept guard as Jesus hung on the cross.

Roman soldiers were always busy.
When they weren't fighting or standing guard, they were building forts
and bridges, supervising in mines
and quarries, or working on road
repairs. So imagine that one of these
soldiers was transferred from roadwork to assisting in the crucifixion of
this self-proclaimed "king." This soldier had heard about Jesus' claims and

> We can know
> about Jesus, hear
> about Him, even
> get close to Him,
> yet miss out on the
> fullness of life He
> came to give us.

rumors of His miracles, but he was completely unaware of the
gravity of this moment on Golgotha. He seemed to be unmoved
by it, focused on doing his job and the possibility of taking home
a seamless robe to sell and make some extra cash. Previously, soldiers had put this purple robe on Jesus to mock Him. Because it
was seamless, it would be worth nothing if they divided it up. So
they rolled dice for it, and this soldier won it, and he was pumped
about going home with something to sell on eBay. Of all the
things that Jesus could have given him that day, he chose Jesus'
robe. He was so close to grace, peace, and joy, but he settled for a
robe. He could have received forgiveness of his sins, purpose for
his life, and redemption.

This is a reminder that we can know about Jesus, hear about
Him, even get close to Him, yet miss out on the fullness of life
He came to give us. This soldier was a foot away from the opportunity to experience God's love, righteousness, and a brand-new
life, but he settled. Don't settle for less than God's best for your

life. It's easy to attend a church and go through the motions, to be physically close to the things of God, but miss out on experiencing the fullness of what Jesus died to provide us. You don't have to limp into Heaven thinking, *Praise God, I made it.* No, we can live a life of victory now. According to Galatians 1:4, Jesus died to deliver and cause us to overcome in this present world, not just the one to come.

God calls us to something wonderful, a life of abundance, a life of victory, yet it's easy to settle for mediocrity along the way, watering down what God has promised. "I hate my job, but it's okay. It's good enough." "My boyfriend isn't everything I was hoping for, but he has all his teeth and has a good job. He's okay." "There's no passion and joy in our marriage, but it's good enough. We get along." "I was hoping to get well, but I've learned to live with it. I'm okay." No, okay is not who you were created to be. Good enough is not what Jesus died to give you.

The enemy can't stop God's plan for your life, but he will do his utmost to convince you to settle for okay along the way. Stir your passion and make up your mind that you won't be talked out of your dream. Refuse to settle for less than God's best. You're not going to water it down, not going to let good enough be good enough. Don't settle for partially free when Jesus can make you fully free. Don't settle for an okay marriage when God has promised you a flourishing one. Don't settle for knowing about Jesus when you can walk with Him. Don't settle for a life chasing things that can't fulfill you when the One who satisfies your soul is closer than the breath you breathe.

Let's learn from the soldier. Let's be people who say, "God, I'm not going to settle. I'm going to keep believing for all You have for me."

Throw Out Your Nets

You may be familiar with this story in Luke 5. "[Jesus] stood by the Lake of Gennesaret, and saw two boats standing by the lake; but the fishermen had gone from them and were washing their nets. Then He got into one of the boats, which was Simon's, and asked him to put out a little from the land. He sat down and taught the multitudes from the boat. When He had stopped speaking, He said to Simon, 'Launch out into the deep and let down your *nets* for a catch.' But Simon answered and said to Him, 'Master, we have toiled all night and caught nothing; nevertheless at Your word I will let down the *net.*' And when they had done this, they caught a great number of fish, and their *net* was breaking. So they signaled to their partners in the other boat to come and help them. And they came and filled both the boats, so that they began to sink" (vv. 1–7 NKJV).

> Are you playing it safe and throwing out only one "net" when God wants to sink your boat?

It's clear that the fishermen had spent the entire night fishing and caught nothing. It's also clear that when Jesus told them to launch into the deep and throw their nets into the same place they had been fishing, Peter was reluctant. I can imagine Peter looking at his crew and saying, "Guys, I know this makes no sense, but just do one net really quick. Let's make this short and sweet." But to all their surprise, fish swarmed into the net to the breaking point. There were so many fish that they had to call in their partners' boat for assistance, and both boats began to sink. Imagine the excitement and thrill. They had never seen anything like that before.

Jesus told the fishermen to let down their "nets." It's interesting that some translations say Peter let down "the net." It's obvious he wasn't expecting much; he had been there and done that. He wasn't expecting many fish, if any.

Are you playing it safe and throwing out only one "net" when God wants to sink your boat? If you would expect, believe, and trust Him for more, I wonder if God wants to sink your boat with blessings, breakthroughs, and victory. I've learned to move beyond get-by prayers and to pray prayers such as, "God, I don't want just half of what You have planned for me; I want all that You have in store for me. I don't want to become half the person You want me to be. I want to become everything You want me to be. Let every gift, talent, and good thing that You've put in me come out to the fullest." In other words, I'm expecting God's best. I'm not just throwing out a net. I'm throwing out as many nets as I have!

What would you catch if you started expecting more? What would happen if you started praying bold prayers? You might catch your husband, or your healing, or the acceptance at the university you feel is right for you. You might catch the promotion you desire or the change in your family that you've been praying about for so long. God has more in store for you. My encouragement is not to settle or let yourself get stuck, but to continue to expect His goodness in your life. Desire His best and not an ounce less!

Real Peace

Over the years I've discovered a common pursuit that all people have, regardless of age, color, or background. It's the pursuit and desire for peace of mind and heart. We all crave to be at peace with ourselves, with who we are, and with where we are in life.

We want to be at peace with what we're doing and where we're going. Maybe you're like me, and you've tried things while hoping they would give you the peace you're looking for. Substances? Vacations? Money? Relationships? Though some can offer a temporary relief or feeling of peace, all of these fade and fall short over time.

My wife and I, Haven and Denver, and our dog, Harley, took a vacation over a spring break to Austin, Texas. Summer's parents flew from Chicago and met us there. We were all very excited to get a much-needed rest, a nice vacation away to experience some peace and quiet. We packed our car and were halfway to Austin when Summer received a call from her dad saying that as he was backing their rental car into the driveway of the vacation lake house, he hit a huge boulder on the side of the driveway. It caused $2,000 worth of damage. I could hear how upset he was on the phone, venting in frustration about having to sort it all out with the rental company. I felt terrible. This was a horrible way to start the vacation.

> We all crave to be at peace with ourselves, with who we are, and with where we are in life.

We arrived later that night, making sure to avoid the boulder as we pulled in. We unpacked and put the kids to bed. At about three o'clock in the morning, I awoke to a splattering sound down the hallway. I got up and walked to the kids' bedroom, where Haven was leaning over the top of the bunk bed rail and throwing up all over the wood floor. She had a 104.5-degree fever. After cleaning the puke off the floor, we tried to settle her, but the fever didn't go down. So we packed her into the car and took her to the

> Your peace doesn't come from changing your location or from the calming of external circumstances. Your peace comes from inside. It comes from the Spirit of God living on the inside of you.

ER. They took good care of her and gave us some medicine to take home. We got back to the house and took the rest of the day to catch up on the sleep we missed.

While we were eating dinner that evening, Denver finished first and was playing with Harley while we were wrapping up. Harley sprinted under the glass dinner table with Denver in hot pursuit.

Unfortunately, Denver didn't realize how far the table edge stuck out. He ran full speed into the side of the glass table. *Bam!* It dropped him instantly. He had this dazed look on his face and a deep cut on his forehead, and he started screaming. So it was back to the ER that we had just been in a few hours before. The nurse saw me coming in and exclaimed, "Wow! What a great start to your vacation, huh?" Rental car smashed, Haven puking, and Denver getting stitches—all in the first twenty-four hours.

On top of all that, two days later, Summer got a flu virus that put her on the couch for the remainder of the trip. What was meant to be a pressure-free, stress-free, relaxing vacation did not turn out to be that way. But this is how life often goes. We plan trips and vacations to try to find peace and rest, only to come back home more exhausted than when we left. (I won't even mention our trip to Disneyland.) Trips are nice. Times we take to get away can be memorable, and we should plan them. But you don't have to take many trips away to discover that they can't give you the permanent peace your soul craves.

There is a story about a group of artists who entered a contest to paint a picture of peace. One artist after another finished their paintings of beautiful sunsets, mountain ranges, and beaches. All of them looked relaxing and calm (like the vacation we had hoped to have). Then the last artist stepped forward and unveiled his painting of a violent storm, rushing floodwaters, lightning, and tree-bending winds. It looked like the opposite of peace. But in the middle of the chaos, tucked away by the side of a rock, was a beautiful white bird at rest. In the midst of all the turmoil, it found peace in the rock. This was true peace, and the painter won first prize.

> You don't have to experience much of life to realize that inner peace can't be found in things—a position, a salary, a relationship, a bottle or pill.

God's will is not that you never have trouble, but that you experience His peace in the midst of it. Peace is not the absence of problems; it's the promise of His presence in the middle of your problems. The good news is that you can stand in the storm of a divorce, sickness, loss, and struggle, and have the peace of God guarding your heart and soul. Your peace doesn't come from changing your location or from the calming of external circumstances. Your peace comes from inside. It comes from the Spirit of God living on the inside of you. It comes when the God of hope fills you "with all joy and peace as you trust in him, so that you may overflow with hope by the power of the Holy Spirit" (Romans 15:13 NIV). You can be at peace, releasing your faith, while God works on your problems.

The Way to Peace

You don't have to experience much of life to realize that inner peace can't be found in things—a position, a salary, a relationship, a bottle or pill. In John 16, Jesus was talking to His disciples, letting them know that this world would never be devoid of reasons to be anxious and overwhelmed, and nothing in it would ever deliver peace to your soul, but He pointed to the answer:

> These things I have spoken to you, that *in Me*, you may have *peace*. (v. 33 NKJV)

In other words, He was saying...

> The peace your soul craves cannot be found in something created.

> This peace is not a feeling or a location.

> This peace cannot be bought or manufactured.

> The world can't give this peace or take it away.

> This peace is found only in Jesus.

> Jesus is the only One who can satisfy your soul and bring the peace that you desire.

This peace is a calm in the storm, a comfort in the chaos, and it goes beyond our understanding.

In the midst of a world that has challenges, problems, and unexpected struggles, where do you go to find your confidence and security? When the flood of uncertainty crashes over you, where do you go to find your inner peace? Jesus is the only One who can satisfy your soul and bring the peace that you desire.

In Luke 23, we read about two criminals who were sentenced to death by crucifixion—the worst-possible life situation. These men were without eternal hope, without peace with God, but they were crucified with the Savior of the world between them. As Jesus hung on the cross, one of the criminals heaped insults on Him, saying, "'If You are the Christ, save Yourself and us.' But the other, answering, rebuked him, saying, 'Do you not even fear God, seeing you are under the same condemnation? Then he said to Jesus, 'Lord, remember me when You come into Your kingdom.' And Jesus said to him, 'Assuredly, I say to you, today you will be with Me in Paradise'" (vv. 39–41 NKJV).

We don't know how much this second criminal knew about Jesus, His teachings, or His miracles, but he'd heard enough to learn that Jesus was acclaimed to be a king who had a kingdom. This man was face-to-face with eternal death, yet in that moment

> The blood of Jesus runs to the hurting, and has the power to give us peace, to restore our brokenness and put us back together.

he believed Jesus was who He said He was. It's interesting that the thief said to Jesus, "Remember me when You come into Your kingdom." In the original Greek text, it says he was adamantly asking Jesus to remember him over and over again: "Remember me! Remember me! Remember me!" In other words, he was verbalizing his spiritual brokenness, that he was lost. His life had fallen apart, but he believed, even in this brief moment, that Jesus could still put it back together. His faith released in that moment saved him. The blood that Jesus was shedding on the cross at that moment saved his soul and brought him to peace with God. As Jesus was being undone physically, He was putting this man back together spiritually!

What do we discover here? The blood of Jesus runs to the

hurting; it has the power to give us peace, restore our broken-ness, and put us back together. Ever run into something in your house? End table? Corner of the bed frame? Nail your shin on something? It's painful. What happens following the run-in? The wounded area usually gets warm, and over time you start to see a bruise forming. What's happening? The blood rushes to the part of the body that has sustained an injury. It rushes to restore, heal, and make it new. A week later, it's gone and you forget you even had an injury! Friends, the blood of Jesus runs with the same pur-pose. The blood of Jesus runs toward what's hurt! He came for the broken and to heal and bind up the broken places in our lives. That's where the blood runs! It runs to the hurting areas of your life. There may be things that you are battling, things that are failing or broken. The good news is that the blood of Jesus can reach those areas and save, heal, restore, and make new! When your faith is released, it activates the power of the cross, the power of the blood of Jesus in your life. Your world may feel as though it's coming apart, but when you choose to put it in God's hands, not only is He capable of putting your life back together, but He can be trusted to keep it together, causing you to live in peace, joy, and victory.

You Can Live the Dream

Livin' the dream is found when you experience the power of the peace of God in your life. True peace is the peace God provides. True peace is the consistent awareness of His presence in your life.

  Jesus says to each of us, "I have come that they may have life, and that they may have it more abundantly" (John 10:10 NKJV). *The Message* says, "I came so they can have real and eternal life, more and better life than they ever dreamed of." The abundant life does not mean the easiest life, but the best life. Following Jesus is not about having the best of everything, but learning to make the best of everything. The promises of "life to the fullest" isn't a promise that everything around you will always be "abundant." It's a promise that peace, joy, and fulfillment begin on the inside. It's a promise that you can enjoy life while God works on you and your problems!

Livin' the dream is another way of saying, "I'm living my life in faith. I'm choosing to have a perspective of faith. I'm seeing my life through the lens of faith, and I'm going to continue to believe that God is in control and that He's working all things for my good. Nothing has to change around me because I have His peace, strength, and joy on the inside!"

You have one life to live. Don't waste another day. God has more for you, a whole lot more. What am I saying? THE DREAM AWAITS.

You can live the dream now.

ACKNOWLEDGMENTS

Writing this book was an incredible journey. It wouldn't have been possible without the wisdom and sacrifice of my wife, Summer, and the encouragement and support of my two beautiful kids, Haven and Denver. The three of you are a dream come true. I thank God every day I get to be your husband and father.

To my literary agent, Shannon Marven at Dupree Miller & Associates. Thank you for believing in me and this message. I appreciate all your hard work and sacrifice.

I am grateful for an incredible team who helped me put this book together for you. Leading them is my FaithWords/Hachette publisher, Daisy Hutton, and my editor, Beth Adams, as well as Patsy Jones, Laini Brown, Cat Hoort, and Kaitlin Mays.

A special thanks to Lance Wubbels for your editorial contributions. You are a brilliant wordsmith, my friend. I appreciate your hard work and diligence to make this the best book possible!

Thanks to my friends and colleagues at Lakewood Church. I get the honor of serving alongside each of you. In many ways, this book is OUR book. Your love, encouragement, and support have helped this project take shape. Thanks for being on my DREAM TEAM.

Thank you to pastors Joel and Victoria Osteen for believing in my dreams. Thank you for showing me what it means to live and lead with character and integrity...and how to work with excellence. Thank you for counting the cost and living your life the way you do. I'm just one of MILLIONS who have been forever changed by you. It's a privilege to be your friend, serve your vision, and LIVE THE DREAM with you! Love you guys!

To my father, Doug Nilson, and mother, Michele McAffee, thank you for teaching me to never quit, to always treat people with love and respect, and to dream BIG. Special thanks to my brother Kris Nilson and sister, Heather Kelley. Your love and loyalty mean the world. Thanks for always being in my corner. To my stepbrother and sister, Brian and Bridget Joseph, thank you for your love and encouragement throughout my life.

Kevin and Debby Schiavo (aka Jack and Dina). Not only did you raise an amazing woman that I now get to call my wife, but you have embraced, encouraged, and loved me like your own son. Thank you for being a consistent source of love and support. I love you guys.

Sincerely,

Greg.

Last but not least, thank you to my big brother, Adam, who passed away on March 5, 2023. You blazed a trail for me that I'm eternally grateful for. You were a brilliant creator in the hands of God, purposed to leave your mark on this world. You've not only left your mark through your art, but you've also left your mark in our hearts, which we will remember and continue to tell the world about. I love you. Your legacy will live on. Until we see each other again...save the bottom bunk in Heaven for me.

ABOUT THE AUTHOR

Nick Nilson is an associate pastor at America's largest church, Lakewood Church. His authenticity and charisma help him share the hope of Jesus everywhere he goes. His work as a leader and communicator has given him the opportunity to help people to realize their full potential in every area of their lives. He is happily married to his wife, Summer, and they pastor at Lakewood Church in Houston, Texas, where they also reside with their children, Haven and Denver, and their spoiled dog, Harley.